Anatomyzing Divinity

Studies in Science, Esotericism and Political Theology

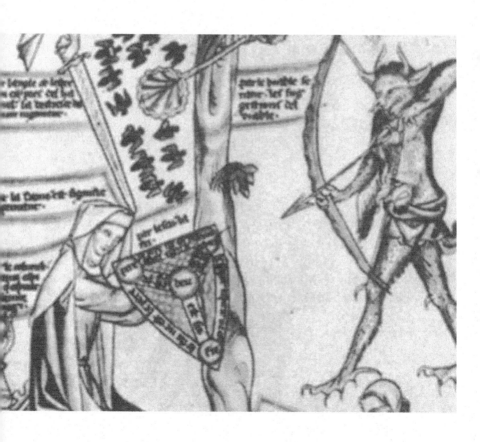

by James L. Kelley

Published by:
Trine Day LLC
PO Box 577
Walterville, OR 97489
1-800-556-2012
www.TrineDay.com
publisher@trineday.net

Library of Congress Control Number: 2011934069

Kelley, James L.
Anatomyzing Divinity: Studies in Science, Esotericism and Political
Theology—1st ed.
p. cm.
Includes bibliography.
Epub (ISBN-13) 978-1-936296-28-6 (ISBN-10) 1-936296-27-6
Kindle (ISBN-13) 978-1-936296-29-3 (ISBN-10) 1-936296-29-2
Print (ISBN-13) 978-1-936296-27-9 (ISBN-10) 1-936296-27-6
1. Alchemy – History 2. Leibniz, Gottfried Wilhelm, – 1646-1716.
3. Philosophy – Monadology – Monads 4. Philip – IV – King of
France – 1268-1314. I. Title

FIRST EDITION
10 9 8 7 6 5 4 3 2 1

Printed in the USA
Distribution to the Trade by:
Independent Publishers Group (IPG)
814 North Franklin Street
Chicago, Illinois 60610
312.337.0747
www.ipgbook.com

For Mary and Zoe

You talk of a body of Divinity, and of Anatomyzing Divinity:
O fine language! But when it comes to triall, it is but a
husk without the kernall; words without life...
— Gerrard Winstanley,
The New Law of Righteousness (1649)[1]

1. *Works of Gerrard Winstanley*, ed. Sabine 234. Cited in J. Andrew Mendelsohn, "Alchemy and Politics in England, 1649-1665," *Past and Present 135* (May 1992): 30-78, at 46.

Contents

Acknowledgments.. x

Foreword by Joseph P. Farrell, D.Phil.(Oxon.)...............xi

Glossary.. xv

Introduction... 1

Part One — The Alchemical Trinity.................................... 39
    Chapter One: The *Magnum Opus* of the Franks............... 43
    Chapter Two: *Anthropos, Cosmos,* and *Theos* According to the Ortho-
    dox Catholic Tradition and the Alchemico-Hermetic Tradition........51
    Chapter Three: The Archetypal Images of the Alchemico-Hermetic
    Tradition.. 59
    Chapter Four: Icons of the Magnum Opus........................ 80
    Conclusion for Part One.. 89

Part Two — "The Man Who Would Be More Than King": Philip
The Fair's Thel-Lemma.. 91
    Chapter Five: An Introduction to Philip the Fair's world........... 93
    Chapter Six: A Case of Arrested Thelemma...................... 99
    Chapter Seven: Political Theology East and West.............. 103
    Conclusion for Part Two.. 109

Part Three — "Scientia Generalis": The Ecumenical Task Of Natural Philosophy According To G.W. Leibniz.................... 117
    Chapter Eight: G.W. Leibniz: Life and Character............ 121
    Chapter Nine: The Development of Leibniz's Science....... 125
    Chapter Ten: Leibniz's Irenicism..................................... 135

Epilogue — Anatomyzing Divinity.................................... 145

Illustrations... 155

Bibliography... 163

Acknowledgements

Much of the research for this volume was conducted at the University of Oklahoma's History of Science Collections. To the Director and Curator of the Collections, Dr. Kerry Mc-Gruder, I offer my deepest thanks. Your contributions to this project run deeper than my paltry words could ever attempt to "anatomyze." Special thanks also to Dr. Van Alan Herd and to Dr. Kathleen Crowther of the University of Oklahoma's History of Science Department. Dr. Crowther honored me by reading and commenting upon portions of this work.

I also wish to thank Damian Russell, Chad McClellan, Roger Johnson and my father Leo Kelley—your insightful comments over the years have contributed much to my understanding of history and theology.

Lastly, the greatest of debts is owed to my spiritual father, Archpriest Anthony Nelson.

To those I have overlooked: Your guidance has been invaluable. It goes without saying that any errors this work contains are solely my own.

Foreword

When Mr. Kelley first contacted me to request that I write a short introduction to this book, I was, of course, honored that he should ask and quite pleased to do so. He informed me that the book would be a collection of essays on various topics of a "Farrellian nature" that would be discussed using a "Farrellian methodology" to discuss them. Besides being intensely curious as to why anyone would choose to write a book on "various topics" using "my" methods of analysis and interpretation, I was also inquisitive as to what those topics would *be,* and which of "my" methods Mr. Kelley would be using to analyze them, for as most people who are familiar with my output know, there are two distinctive sets of books that I have written, one group, from long ago, being a purely academic series of theological writings and analysis, and the other being a grouping of purely speculative books on topics that may best be described as "alternative science and history," the sorts of books one normally finds in bookstores under the heading "New Age" or even "conspiracy." What most people seem unaware of is that, at least in my mind and intentions, both sets of books were meant to be connected, and indeed, I have left clues throughout all the books that they are to be so connected. How, I will not say, for that is for my readership to figure out.

But these considerations only intensified my curiosity: which series or set of books did Mr. Kelley mean here?

Much to my delighted surprise – one might say even *shock* – when the actual chapters of Mr. Kelley's book arrived in an email attachment a few days later, I discovered that he meant *both* sets, that he, almost alone of all my readers, had not only read both series of books, but had done what I intended from the outset and made certain detailed and quite specific connections *between* them. This is particularly evident in the introduction and in the first chapter of this work, where Mr. Kelley connected my thoughts and analyses of alchemy and its

Hermetic roots from the second series of books, to some specifically academic and theological analyses of Western European Christian culture that I made long ago in my first set of books.

"Finally!" I thought to myself as I read that first chapter, "someone has figured out what I'm up to! Someone has connected the dots correctly! Someone has begun to see the implications!"

But even more to my delighted surprise, Mr. Kelley had not stopped there, merely drawing connections from clues interspersed throughout my own books, but he had taken those connections and methodology and gone on to draw out even more implications in two fascinating chapters, one the philosophy of Leibniz and another on King Philip the Fair of Medieval France.

In addition to the virtues of this book's content, Mr. Kelley argues his thesis with an engaging and entertaining style of composition, and I am even tempted to say that it is elegant, as is evinced through his judicious use of rhetorical techniques. His prose is about heady, heavy topics to be sure, but it never becomes labored or ponderous; there is an elasticity and classical grace to it that draws the reader in, moving him smoothly from one insight and implication to the next. This will become particularly evident to the reader in the Leibniz section.

Mr. Kelley has seen some of the connections between the two series of my own output, has seen many of the almost endless implications of those connections, and has made them his own, adding new methods of analysis, drawing out new implications, sending me back to my own sources for further reflection. Do not, therefore, let the apparent "shortness" or "thinness" of this book deceive you, for I rather suspect that the reader will, like me, find himself drawn to read it again and again, or thinking about its contents at the oddest moments. It is, in the final analysis, one of those books that one never stops reading, but only puts down or "finishes," if only to pause and think about.

Mr. Kelley has laid out an elegant banquet here, neither too much food, nor too little, but the tempered and just amount. Enjoy!

Joseph P. Farrell, D.Phil.(Oxon.)
Spearfish, South Dakota
2010

Glossary

Adoptionism: The heretical belief that Christ was merely a man until he was adopted by God the Father at His baptism. This heresy first surfaced in the 2nd century A.D.

aither: Though commonly thought of as the "upper air" that surrounded the Olympian milieu, the researches of Peter Kingsley have shown that aither was a term often used to mean "mist" or "water transmuting into air."

Alchemy: An experimental science with strong mystical motivations and content that began in the first century A.D. in Egypt. Around the same time, or perhaps slightly earlier, a strongly similar (if not identical) science became evidenced in China. The science of alchemy is not merely the quest to transmute ignoble metals such as lead, iron, and copper, into noble metals—silver and gold, though this is the definition with which most studies of the subject begin. It must be noted, however, that alchemy varies greatly depending upon the time and place in history in which it is practiced, and thus it defies any brief summation.

Alexander the Great (356-323 B.C.): King of Macedon and son of Philip II of Macedon. Conquered the Persian Empire, Egypt, and Greece. During his brief time in Egypt, Alexander founded the city of Alexandria, the site of alchemy's beginning.

Anhypostatic: From Greek "an-" meaning "without," and "hypostasis," meaning person. In the patristic writings, anhypostatic means a thing or a state conceived of as totally separated from personal existence. Gnostics and Hermeticists of various stripes have striven to deny the patristic categories of person, energy, and essence by introducing the notion of anhypostatic energies. The alchemical idea of "soul essence" or prima materia fits well with the Gnoseo-Hermetic idea of a cosmic force—the energy of the world soul or the Anthropos—that, since it spans all human persons and all other non-sentient beings, cannot be rigidly defined as hypostatic.

Animism: From latin anima, "soul, life". The belief that spirit exists in all forms of nature.

Apophasis: Negation. From the Greek apophanai, meaning "to deny." The term refers to a mode of theologizing that uses words to refer to realities that cannot be circumscribed by concepts or terms.

Augustine of Hippo, Bl. (354-430): Bishop of Hippo Regius in North Africa, Aurelius Augustinus, better known as Blessed Augustine, either wittingly or unwittingly constructed a new Christian tradition that had as its central feature a melding of Late Antique Platonic philosophy with the original Christian Tradition that he inherited. St. Augustine's theology has no real rival in the West; he has formed the Western mind—both Christian and non-Christian—more directly and more pervasively than perhaps any other thinker. Augustine has had no discernable influence upon Eastern Orthodox dogma, which directly condemns many theological positions held by the great African writer.

Bacon, Roger (ca. 1214 – ca. 1292): A Franciscan friar whose theories on optics and alchemy caused controversy after the 1240s. Bacon is significant through his early use of alchemy as a central component of a grand ecumenical strategy to convert the world to the Roman Catholic Church, a plan that involved the unlikely combination of gigantic mirrors and humor-regulating elixirs.

Boyle, Robert (1627-1691): Natural philosopher best known for "Boyle's Law." His work, though rooted in alchemical traditions, laid the groundwork for modern chemistry.

Brahman: The Hindu concept of the Supreme Reality.

Carolingian Dynasty: A Frankish noble family whose line of kings included Charlemagne (d. 814 A.D.) and Louis the Pious (778-840 A.D.).

Cataphasis: Affirmation. In Christian theology, cataphasis often refers to the use of language to make positive assertions about God, or at least about the effects of the actions of God.

Chalcedonian Orthodoxy: The Faith upheld at the Fourth Ecumenical Council, held near Constantinople at Chalcedon in 451 A.D. The core of the Chalcedonian teaching was that Christ had both a divine and a human nature, though He remained one.

Copula: A link between two things; a middle term.

Daoism (also Taoism): A tradition of philosophical and religious thought that traces its origin to ancient Chinese society and to its traditional founder, Lao-Tzu. The emphasis is on following the Dao ("the Way"), which is both the origin of the cosmos and the harmony that constitutes it.

Democritus of Abdera (ca. 460 – ca. 370 B.C.): A Greek philosopher born in Thrace who speculated that all reality is composed of atoms. He also taught that the soul is made up of incredibly fine spherical atoms, and that these soul-atoms were somehow akin to the element fire. Later ancient writers put Democritus's name on many mystical, magical, and alchemical treatises, most notably the *Physika kai Mystika*, an adapted excerpt from which is found above, in this book's introduction.

Docetism: The belief that Christ's body was an illusion. From the Greek "dokeo," to seem.

ecumenism: Ecumenism is often referred to as the conviction, embodied in various programmes and/or strategies of religious diplomacy, that either 1) many discrete religious groups are, on an inner level, already in communion, or 2) that all religions in the world are, in a "spiritual" sense already teaching the same thing, and thus should cultivate a greater awareness of this unity or even work toward the actual ecclesiastical intercommunion of all religious institutions. No one knows when such ideas began, but the Persians as well as the Greeks and Romans made it a point to search out foreign gods and teachings and to find the wisdom in them.

Empedocles (ca. 492 – ca. 432 B.C.): Mystic and philosopher from Acragas in Sicily who authored two poems, On Nature and Purifications, fragments of which have survived. He is known for, among other things, introducing the notion of four elements—earth, water, air, and fire—as the basic "roots" or constituents of matter.

Eunomianism: A stripe of extreme Arianism that declared Christ to be of a different nature than His Father. Named after Eunomius, bishop of Cyzicus (4th cen. A.D.), who also held that man could know the essence of God with the same intimacy and precision that he could know mental concepts.

Farrell, Joseph P.: A Patristics scholar who graduated with a Doctorate from Pembroke College, Oxford University and who was born in Sioux Falls, South Dakota. Farrell's significance lies in his astounding combination of insights from various disciplines, an example being his notion that some ancient texts such as the Corpus Hermeticum and the Enuma Elish contain scientific ideas only recently rediscovered by modern physicists. His early works, though more strictly theological in nature, are seen by some to be significant though unacknowledged contributions to the history of ideas in the West.

Filioque: Latin for "and the Son." The Latin word was inserted into the Nicene-Constantinopolitan Creed around 500 A.D., changing the original "the Holy Spirit, Who proceeds from the Father," to "the Holy Spirit, Who proceeds from the Father and the Son (*Filioque*)." This interpolation was opposed by Christians in the Eastern Roman Empire, both before the Great Schism (1054) and after, up to the present day.

Geber: (also "Pseudo-Geber" or "Ps.-Geber"): The name modern scholars have given to an anonymous European alchemist who flourished in the 13th cen. A.D. "Geber" is the Latin form of "Jabir ibn Hayyan," an influential Islamic alchemist (8th cen. A.D.).

Gnosticism: In its narrow sense, the term Gnosticism refers to a number of heretical Christian groups that are identified as early as the late 1st century A.D. These groups' teachings often include 1) belief that only a few humans are predestined to return to their maker, the rest being lower creatures, 2) the cosmos is a fallen realm of illusion that imprisons those without knowledge of the immaterial, most-high god, and 3) those in the Christian Church who lack the higher knowledge, including the clergy, are in the most important sense victims of deception, since there is a higher god than the lower one they worship. Gnosticism in its wide sense refers to certain features of the mystical and theurgic worldviews held by many during the first few centuries of our era (and also held by many in every epoch since Late Antiquity, even in our present day, i.e. the New Age movement). Aspects of Gnosticism as a broad spiritual tendency include (depending upon which scholar is doing the enumerating): 1) belief in a sharp opposition between the spiritual and the material in man and in the cosmos, 2) emphasis on direct intuition from a transcendent deity to the spirit or *nous* of man, and an attendant de-valuation of rationalistic knowledge and ecclesiastical structures, and 3) the borrowing and altering of religious myths, texts, and images from established traditions, most prominently that of Orthodox Christianity. It must here be noted that some Gnostic groups formed their own hierarchies and thus were totally separate from the Orthodox Catholic Church. Others who stayed in the Church were censured and/or excommunicated.

Great Work, the (Magnum Opus): The science of alchemical transformation.

Helvetic Confessions: Two documents containing the confession of faith of the Reformed churches of Switzerland. Both were drafted in the 16th century.

Heraclius (ca. 575 – 641 A.D.): Eastern Roman Emperor (610-641 A.D.), who probably initiated the "theme" system of military organization in Anatolia, and who attempted to introduce dogmatic compromise between the Orthodox Church and the group(s) of Oriental Orthodox who held that Christ has one nature (a theology commonly known as Monophysitism, a term which is not accepted by these groups).

Hermeneutics: The study of the theory and practice of interpretation.

Hermes Trismegistus, or "Thrice-Great Hermes": Hermes Trigmegistus is described in many documents from Late Antiquity as the founder of alchemy and the bringer of civilization to the Egyptians and later the Greeks.

hermeticism: A mystical philosophy (also known as hermetism) that is associated with the so-called Corpus Hermeticum, a group of Greek texts dating from the first few centuries A.D. These texts are mainly dialogues between a Hermetic seeker (sometimes identified as Hermes Trigmegistus, or "Hermes the Thrice-Holy") and a divine figure. The divine figure instructs the seeker on how to purify himself so as to ascend past the planetary spheres and their demonic rulers or "archons." The final goal of this hermetic quest is union with the divine, which is often spoken of as the mortal seeker becoming a god. Anoine Faivre has spoken of hermeticism as the "theory" behind magic, astrology, and various forms of theurgy. Faivre also saw hermeticism's view of the cosmos as a vast system of indirect connections that were explored through an expanding of the individual seeker's consciousness.

Hypostasis: Greek for "person."

Iatrochemistry: A tradition of medicinal chemistry that has its roots in alchemy and which was practiced by Paracelsus in the 16th century.

Irenicism: From the Greek word meaning "peace," irenicism usually refers to any Christian theological orientation that seeks unity between disparate religious believers on the basis of some rationalistic principle or principles.

Joachim of Fiore (ca. 1135-12-2): Founder of the order of San Giovanni in Fiore, Joachim was born in Calabria. He believed that a new age was at hand that would see the rise of a new, inner Church of ultra-Cistercians. Incredibly, Joachim believed that this Age of the Spirit (to be reached in 1260 A.D.) would feature the new Church's direct contact with God and the inauguration of total freedom on the Earth. Joachim may have been the very first ecclesiastical writer to spark widespread belief in an earthly "thousand year reign."

Late Antiquity: The period of time that marked the end of Classical Antiquity and the beginning of the Middle Ages. Usually this transitional epoch is thought to span from about 100 A.D. to around 600 or so A.D. In this study, we are including the first century A.D. under the "Late Antique" rubric, and we will also reach back as many as two or three centuries before the time of Christ to highlight texts and events that presaged spiritual and social developments which blossomed into the mystical soup that was Late Antiquity.

Leibniz, G.W. (1646-1716): A German mathematician, philosopher, and ecumenist whose greatest contribution to the modern world is his invention (developed independently from Isaac Newton, but at approximately the same time!) of the infinitesimal calculus. He also improved and rethought the binary number system that is a foundation stone for computers and thus for virtually all modern technological developments. Chapter Three of this study hopes to cast a spotlight on Leibniz's lifelong struggle to develop an effective strategy for uniting the Lutheran Church with other Protestant groups and especially with the Roman Catholic Church. The most interesting and unexpected aspect of Leibniz's irenicist quest its reliance upon mystical concepts, teachings, and models that can be traced back to Hermeticism and to Gnosticism.

Madhihassan, Syed (1892-): A Pakistani chemist and historian of ideas whose hundreds of published works explore various aspects of alchemy and esotericism.

Mandorla: An ancient symbol that consists in two interlocking circles whose overlap creates an almond-shaped third section.

Maria the Jewess: An early alchemist who was a student of Zosimus of Panopolis. The bain-marie, a kind of double boiler that keeps water in an interior basin at a consistent temperature through heating water contained in a second basin in a surrounding vessel, was named after her.

Middle Ages (Medieval Period): The period between about 500 or 600 A.D. and ca. 1500 A.D. featuring—in Europe—a feudal society of mainly farming and shepherding peasants and aristocratic knights and lords. The high culture of the Classical period was replaced with a Church-centered culture that looked to the Papal States and later to the Frankish Emperor as guides. In the Eastern Roman Empire, this time period saw imperial expansion and later collapse, as Islamic Civilization ended the viability of the Roman Empire in the East in the sixteenth century.

Millenarianism: The belief in an immanent, all-encompassing transformation of life. Usually a 1,000 year cycle is operative in the notion.

Monophysitism: The Christian heresy that believes Christ has one nature after the Incarnation.

In Frankish medieval political theory, the king was seen as being, in some sense, one with Christ. Also, the king was seen to be a wielder of military and spiritual power. The political theory behind this Frankish Christ-king was traced back to Nestorian and Monophysite theological writings by Ernst Kantorowicz, leading the latter to speak of a royal "monophysitism" in the medieval West.

Nag Hammadi Scrolls: A collection of early Chrsitian Gnostic texts discovered near the Egyptian town of Nag Hammadi in 1945.

Nestorianism: The teaching—named after its purveyor Nestorius, Patriarch of Constantinope from 428 to 431 A.D.—that Christ's humanity and His divinity are two separate persons that forge a contractual agreement to be one, this pairing being put forth as the meaning of the Son of God's Incarnation as Jesus Christ. Condemned as heresy at the 3rd and 4th Ecumenical Councils of the Orthodox Catholic Church (5th century A.D.).

nous: Though often mistranslated as "mind," nous is a Greek word that means the deepest inner personal existence of man, his or her "spiritual mind." The ancient Greeks had conflicting ideas about anthropology, at times declaring the physical body to be a filthy prison—"soma sema," meaning "body tomb." At other times, as reflected in the figure of the iatromantis, the Greeks viewed man holistically, as a single undivided bodysoul (my term).

Ockhamists: Followers of William of Ockham, Medieval theologian who, as a nominalist, believed that only individuals exist. Consequently, William held that there were no Augustino-Platonic universals.

Osiris: The Egyptian god of the dead, the afterlife, and fertility. Husband and brother of Isis, Osiris is killed and dismembered by the evil god Set, though Isis revives him and bears the deity Horus, who avenges his father by defeating Set. The figure of Osiris ties together ancient fertility rites and king cults with the esoteric sciences that included alchemy and which blossomed in the first centuries A.D. Many esoteric Greek and Egyptian texts name Osiris, Isis, and Set as the three sides of a 3-4-5 triangle, the figure used in the so-called Pythagorean Theorem. Horus was the hypotenuse, the holy progeny of the Father and his Consort, the triangle representing the divine harmony of the cosmos, which is also a dynamic force that unfolds and, though divine, actually expands and grows!

Orphism: A set of mystical religious texts and esoteric practices that date back to the time of Pythagoras, many Orphic writings purportedly being from the Samian's own pen. Orphism emphasized a religious initiation that served to safeguard the initiate's journey to the heavenly realm after death. Many intriguing but maddeningly inconclusive tangents with Pythagoreanism rear their heads to any who investigate Orphic texts: Both Orphics and Pythagoreans emphasize asceticism, spiritual fatherhood under a guru, and vegetarianism, not to mention a similar cosmology shot through with an ambiguous dualism. Music and song, true to the movement's namesake, are also important to Orphics, as they are to Pythagoras and his followers.

Parmenides (circa 500 B.C.): A Greek philosopher and mystic born in Elea in southern Italy. He founded the Eleatic school of philosophy and wrote the philosophical poem *On Nature*, the first part of which aimed to show that change is impossible and that there is only one substance.

Philip IV (the Fair): King of France 1285-1314

Philosopher's Stone: A miraculous substance thought to be able to transmute base metals into gold. Often alchemists saw the creation of the philosopher's stone (also called "elixir") as their immediate goal, since its production allows one to repeatedly transmute metals, presumably instantaneously.

Plotinus (ca. 204 – 270 A.D.): Platonic philosopher whose Enneads outlined a detailed metaphysics centered upon the cosmos as an emanation from the One and other divine intermediaries.

Polyhistor, Lucius Cornelius Alexander (1st cen. B.C.): A Greek scholar whose prolific output as a writer earned him the name polyhistor. His work comes down to us only in fragments.

prima materia (also *materia prima*): Latin for "first source" or "primary matter." In alchemical theory, prima materia is the utterly simple substance that contains every quality and manifestation in potentia. Some alchemist's saw their task as a retracing of matter's path of differentiation back to the original undifferentiated prime matter.

Primus Inter Pares: Latin for "first among equals."

Pythagoras of Samos (ca. 570-495 B.C.): A scientist and a mystic philosopher from Ionia who formed a sect with political ambitions in the 6th cen. B.C. in his native Samos and later in Croton (Southern Italy). Pythagoras saw all of creation as a product of the "elements of numbers." This theological doctrine seemed to teach that the proportion or relationships amongst the various physical bodies (and the unseen spiritual harmony that undergirds these relationships), a unity based upon certain contrary yet complementary cosmo-divine forces and their development, is divine and is the goal of all human striving.

Scutum Fidei: Latin for "Shield of Faith."

Taiquing: "Great Clarity," the goal of the Chinese alchemy that developed in China and elsewhere in the Far East in the 2nd cen. B.C. and thereafter.

Telos: Greek for "goal" or "predetermined end."

Thelema: Greek for "will."

Yates, Frances A.: (1899-1981): A British historian whose works broke with traditional history writing by concentrating on occult philosophy and its influence upon scientists and other prominent thinkers from the Renaissance to the present.

Zosimos of Panopolis (3rd-4th cen. A.D.): An alchemist as well as a Gnostic philosopher born in Panopolis (present day Akhmim) in Egypt ca. 300 A.D. He was perhaps the first to present a detailed picture of alchemical practice that was fully-fleshed out both as a chemical and a spiritual endeavor.

INTRODUCTION

The learned one Democritus spoke these words concerning his experiences in Egypt:

After learning these things from my master and aware of the diversity of the matter, I set myself to make the combination of the natures. But, as our master had died before our initiation was completed and we were still all taken up in learning the matter, it was from Hades, as one says, that I tried to evoke him. I applied myself to the task, and, as soon as he appeared, I apostrophised him in these terms, "Are you going to give me nothing in return for what I have done for you?"

I spoke in vain. He kept silent.

However when I addressed him as well I could and asked him how I should combine the natures, he told me that it was difficult for him to speak; the *daimon* wouldn't allow it. He said only, 'The books are in the temple.'

Turning back, I then went to make searches in the temple on the chance of being able to lay my hands on the books, [for] he had taken precautions before dying that no one should know of the books except his son on reaching maturity.....

But despite all our searching we found nothing; and so we gave ourselves a terrible lot of trouble in *trying to learn how substances and natures were united and combined in a single substance*. Well, when we had realized the synthesis of matter, some time passed by and a festival was held in the temple. We took part, all of us, in a banquet.

Then, as we were in the temple, all of a sudden a column of its own accord opened up in the middle. But at first glance there seemed nothing inside. However, [our master's son] told us that it was in this column his father's books had been placed. And taking charge of the situation, he brought the thing out into the open. But when we bent to look, we saw in surprise that nothing had escaped us except this wholly valuable formula which we found there. *"One nature delights in another nature; one nature conquers another nature; one nature over-rules another nature."* Great was our admiration for the way he had concentrated in a few words all the Scripture.

I cannot suppress a good-hearted chuckle as I wonder what you, dear reader, will make of this curious passage.1 Its language and its setting suggest something between a Nag Hammadi scroll and a Hassidic folk tale. Think of the texture of the acolyte's coarse linen robe, the smell of incense (not the wretchedness peddled at New Age bead shops, but the kind of thing an old Bedouin's spice box would reek of).

Now that you have a few sensory and literary reference points, here's an adjectival peg upon which to hang them: "mystical."

Though for some the term may bring to mind either a peruke-pated Freemason or a bug-eyed Aleister Crowley, we should not allow these modern associations to cancel out the original meaning of the word "mystical." The term originated as the Greek *mystike*, meaning simply "hidden" or "secret."

Anyway, back to our odd little tale of Democritus and the Egyptian guru. This writing comes from the ancient world; that is, before 500 A.D. But, if this is an ancient mystical text, and if mystical means hidden, then what is being hidden?

1. The quotation is Jack Lindsay's translation of a passage from *Physika kai Mystika* (see his *Origins of Alchemy in Graeco-Roman Egypt* [New York: Barnes and Noble, Inc., 1970], 102-103) slightly modified, as in the added emphasis, the introductory tag line (also added by author), and the phrase "One nature delights...," for which I used C. Anne Wilson's translation in her *Philosophers, Iōsis and Water of Life* (Leeds: W.S. Maney and Son Ltd., 1984), 3. For the original Greek text and a French translation of *Physika kai Mystika*, see Marcelin Berthelot, *Collection des anciens alchemists grecs*, 4 vols. (Paris: Steinheil, 1887-8), 2.43 [Hereafter cited as CAAG].

In the ancient world, knowledge (Gr. *gnosis*) was often associated with exclusionary social, religious, or clan groups. These organizations, the world's earliest craft guilds, often required existing and/or prospective members to undergo initiations. These ceremonies were religious in nature, and this spiritual orientation was evinced in every aspect of these groups' craft or other activities. Though craftsmen's handbooks were not unknown—some of which we will be examining in this study—such rare examples of written gnosis were not for public consumption. Some were accompanied by dire warnings, such as the Babylonian text that cautions: "The young priest may see these rites which you perform, but the stranger who does not possess the hereditary knowledge of the rites shall not see them, unless he wishes his days to be shortened."[2] Thus, in the ancient milieu, it was common for texts pertaining to knowledge to be jealously guarded by the groups that produced them. In fact these exclusionary groups' organizational structure was based upon 1) a strict code of secrecy; 2) the separation between those who have been initiated into guild insiders and uninitiated outsiders; 3) a spiritual, even familial bond between master and apprentice; and 4) the preservation of specialized knowledge with a concomitant way of life characterized throughout by intertwined practical and spiritual aspects and applications.

With these points in mind, let us recount the gist of our mysterious text: A master craftsman and mage named Democritus journeys to Egypt, where he comes under the tutelage of an unnamed guru, who teaches the neophyte about the inner principles of matter and the "combination of (material) natures." The guru has a "son," here indicating a star pupil or intermediate student, who is in line to receive the esoteric teachings of the guru, but before this arcane tuition can be passed on—alas!—the teacher perishes. An undeterred Democritus *invokes the*

---

2. Sidney H. Hooke, *Babylonian and Assyrian Religion* (Norman, OK: University of Oklahoma Press, 1963), 125. Cit. in Thomas McEvilley, *The Shape of Ancient Thought: Comparative Studies in Greek and Indian Philosophies* (New York: Allworth Press, 2002), 80.

dead man's spirit from Hades, though he is opposed by a demon. Next we find our seeker in an Egyptian temple—the occasion a "banquet," doubtless some sort of religious ceremony—where a pillar splits open, revealing the books of the departed holy man. In this precious cache is found the entrancing proverb about the sympathy, antipathy, and overpowering of natures vis-à-vis natures. Though we, dewy-eyed onlookers, perhaps do not yet grasp the significance of this saying, our Democritus and his companion certainly *do* know, directly and intuitively, that *their master's chemical key is nothing less than the divine wisdom they have spent their lives seeking.* So, dear reader, what do you make of our eldritch text?

You may be surprised to learn that these few paragraphs are from an ancient alchemical tract. In fact, you have just read a passage from one of the earliest (and most influential) alchemical texts in existence: The *Physika kai Mystika* of Democritus, which was written about 200 B.C. in Egypt.[3]

Alchemy[4] sprang into existence during the first centuries of the Christian era, when the trade networks and population shifts associated with the expansion of the Roman Empire encouraged or forced a large number of ethnic and social groups into cramped urban centers such as Alexandria and Rome. Recall Pliny the Younger's comment that the Christians were numerous in the city of Rome because every wicked and dangerous sect and persuasion finds its way into the city, where it tries its luck and sometimes succeeds. As for Alexandria, I be-

---

3. The scholarly consensus is that "Democritus" is not the author of *Physika kai Mystika*, though no one has, in my mind, brought forth any convincing evidence that proves exactly who the author was. Regardless, I have refrained from entering into this obscure scholarly controversy, though I agree that Democritus of Abdera (see Glossary entry) was not the author. One advantage to foregoing any fruitless (for our purposes) discussion of the authorship of the *Physika* will be our avoiding confusing and unwieldy names such as "pseudo-Democritus" or "Ps.-Democritus." For a discussion of some of the issues involved in the *Physika* authorship question, see Jackson P. Hershbell, "Democritus and the Beginnings of Alchemy," *Ambix* 34.1 (March 1987): 5-20.
4. Actually, the term "alchemy" comes from *al-kimiya*, an Arabic term for the Greek *chumeia*, the latter's meaning being hotly contested by many scholars, but which most likely means something like "art of transmutation."

lieve it impossible that anyone, myself included, can comprehend fully the uniqueness of this late antique jewel. Moreover, I am certain that Alexandria, with its temples, libraries, and commercial complexes, contrasted even more with her neighboring hamlets than does any modern metropolis vis-à-vis its outlying towns. Because of this and many other reasons, it is an arduous task for a historian to untie the Gordian Knot of "isms" that wafted like incense through the air of the Late Roman world, a scene replete with cosmopolitan ports and flavor-of-the-week religions. However, we are aided in our task by the fact that, whatever number of confusing and seemingly conflicting influences seemed to weigh down and otherwise saturate these late antique writers' letters, handbooks and treatises, they all had one thing in common: these writers *did more than simply write, they put their alphabet soup of spells, recipes and prayers into practice in temples and laboratories.* Thus, we have a more-or-less liturgical constant, a handing down of various occult traditions of knowledge and ritual practice that served as a force of continuity amid the shifting sands of the early centuries A.D.

In the neck of the Roman woods upon which we will focus—Northern Egypt—there were a number of groups from various intellectual and religious backgrounds, some exhibiting features of the above described craft fraternities. A few of the groups who contributed something—however indefinable—to the late antique Alexandrian milieu were:

> 1) *societies of Egyptian priests*, many if not all of whom were craftsmen who had to find ways to supply the almost endless demand for gold cult objects for the Dionysian ceremonies that became popular after the age of Alexander the Great.[5] The few early gold- and silver-making recipes we have found (which either show how to plate alloys of base metals with noble coatings, or simply instruct the craftsman on how to create alloys that gleam with noble hues) were doubtless used by these priests, many of whom—to

---

5. Wilson, *Iōsis*, 11.

judge by the recipe texts—were not ignorant of or averse
to Hermetic and Gnostic religious notions. Zosimos of Panopolis (3rd-4th cen. A.D.), who recommended a kind of
incubatory spiritual meditation as a necessary preparation
for any kind of metallurgical or other craft-oriented work,
was himself probably a high-ranking Egyptian initiate;[6]

2) *associations of craftsmen*, which appear to have been,
in some ways, a cross between a Greek mystery cult and
an ancient craft guild. We are certain that within ancient
craft culture the forge was considered to be a fearful locus
of power. In fact, the ceremonies performed by these craftsmen to render the forge safe for use sometimes involved
human (even infant) sacrifice. The forger felt that he was in-
terfering with the natural ripening of base metals into noble
ones, and that the god(s) of the craft had to be appeased or
otherwise dealt with before any transmutation could take
place.[7] Some scholars have pointed to the forger's invention
of cupellation—a process in which a mass of silver ore or
other type of ore is heated, causing the ignoble metals to
be separated from the precious ones—as a major break-
through in the direction of alchemy, since forgers seem to
have thought that they were *creating* silver and gold;[8] and

3) *Pythagoreans*. For now, I am lumping together
under this rubric anyone in Egypt who claimed to be
following the teachings of Pythagoras of Samos (ca. 570-
495 B.C.).[9] The next few pages will include a few words
concerning the Pythagorean influence upon the early
alchemical writings. Let it be said here that Pythagoreans were an ascetic religio-political society founded by
Pythagoras himself in the Ionian city of Samos and later
in Croton, which is in Southern Italy.

---

6. On "incubation" as a spiritual technique in Ancient Greece and in the Hellenized world of Late Antiquity, see Peter Kingsley, *In the Dark Places of Wisdom*
(Inverness, CA: The Golden Sufi Center, 1999).
7. H.G. Sheppard, "Alchemy: Origin or Origins?" *Ambix* 17.2 (July 1970): 69-84, at
80.
8. Vladimir Karpenko, "The Chemistry and Metallurgy of Transmutation," *Ambix*
39.2 (July 1992): 47-62, at 50.
9. Later in this introduction, I will use the term "Pythagoreans" to indicate the
members of the sect of Pythagoras as well as any who came after him who
claimed to be his follower.

Medieval woodcut depicting Pythagoras of Samos playing musical instruments tuned to Pythagorean scales.

Now, instead of doing the expected thing—trudging through lists of arid facts in the hopes of *defining* alchemy—I would like instead to linger just a bit upon the surreal text with which we began, the one purportedly written by Democritus known as the *Physika*. If we do not first get some kind of feel for the texture of late antiquity, we will not gain any insight into our subject, but rather will be left with a useless string of names and dates.

First of all, we should note the decidedly *Egyptian* flavor of the material. Democritus is hanging around Egyptian temples, and he is calling up his guru—probably a member of an association of Egyptian temple prelates—from an Osirean slumber. Plus, it is remarkable that Democritus' description of his life as a spiritual child of a once-living spiritual master who, aside from his other abilities, appears far from ignorant of matters chemical and metallurgical—has the feel of an initiation into a Greek mystery cult, with its torchlit "banquet," strict code of secrecy, and even an *epoptai* (the so-called "showing" of a sacred object in a mystery cult initiation) of sorts in the sudden revelation of the guru's writings in the pillar. Let us not forget that this "hidden book in temple" theme was common to alchemical, Hermetic, astrological, as well as mystery cult literature, and that the *Physika*—a kind of archetypal alchemical source—features the revelation of the sacred text in a specifically Egyptian initiation ritual is, in and of itself, significant.

It is important to note that this exotic birthplace for alchemy—a dark corner in an Egyptian temple in Alexandria—with its very idiosyncratic set of religio-philosophical reference points, fades quickly from the minds of later scholars who would rather see in the origins of chemistry an outgrowth of "Greek rationalism" rather than an offshoot of obscure cultic practice. These scholars usually put down their stakes in Renaissance soil, from whence they glance back at a supposedly non-mystical Medieval alchemy, though they quickly wheel around to the seventeenth century, where one can find comfort in the skeptical chemistry of Robert Boyle. From this dubious vantage point, the Renaissance appears a momentary spasm of mystical ecstasy that can be of little real interest since the Renaissance alchemist (so their logic follows) was not the sought after proto-scientist, but more of a mystical crank.

Since I will quite belabor the point later on, let me briefly assert here that *this idea of alchemy as, at its core, a strictly "scientific" endeavor (in the modern sense of the word) is, as one writer recently put it, a "scandal" of scholarship, since the distinguishing mark of alchemy in every era is its dual focus upon what is going on in the lab and what is going on in the soul of the alchemist.*[10] Our later examination of many more alchemical texts will easily prove this point, which, like many other important facts of history, would be obvious, were it not for the unbelievable hubris of the scholarly voices that gainsay it.

That the foregoing thumbnail sketch of what I call the "grand alchemical narrative"—alchemy as non-mystical proto-science—is a gross distortion should already be apparent. What is less obvious is the connecting line between this historiographical fiction and the pop-culture image of alchemy, the latter being the one I myself held when I first started researching this fascinating topic. Before I actually got my scholarly elbows dirty tracking down the primary texts of early alchemy—those mainly of Greco-Egyptian provenance—I imagined that alchemy most likely took shape somewhere on the Eastern border of Germany in some Teutonic Faust's castle or perhaps a German monastery library's basement filled with blackened-faced friars; so I mused early on, doubtless influenced by modern day novels and films. To be certain, alchemy carried on and even flourished in Medieval Europe—and we examine this history in Chapter 1—but its genesis lay in an earlier time far removed from the fiefdoms, castles, lords, and bishops of later European history.

Actually, though the term "alchemy" was coined in Medieval Europe, originally it was variously referred to as the "Sacred Art" or "Great Work," or some such grandiose label,[11] and

---

10. George-Florin Călian, "Alkimia Operativa and Alkimia Speculativa: Some Modern Controversies On the Historiography of Alchemy," *Annual of Medieval Studies at CEU* 16 (2010): 166-190, at 178.

11. Paul T. Keyser, "Alchemy in the Ancient World: From Science to Magic," *Illinois Classical Studies* 15 (1990): 353-378, at 353: "'Alchemy' is the anglicised Byzantine name given to what its practitioners referred to as 'the Art' (techne) or 'Knowledge' (episteme), often characterised as divine (Theia), sacred (hiera) or mystic (mystike)."

began, as far as we can tell, as a mystical science or holy craft in Hellenized Egypt around the 1st century A.D. The goal of the craft, it is agreed by most scholars, was twofold: 1) to change baser metals into silver and gold, and 2) to achieve the personal salvation of the craftsman. Fabrizio Pregadio makes the following apt comments about the Sacred Art's origin:

> On the one hand, the techniques for refining and transmuting minerals and metals do not constitute alchemy per se, as they do not necessarily imply the existence of a doctrinal and soteriological background [since] the techniques may come to be transmitted separately from it. (-) On the other hand, the doctrinal principles at the basis of the compounding of the [alchemical] elixirs are shared by alchemy with other traditions and disciplines.... (-) Alchemy, in other words, cannot be defined either by its techniques or by its doctrinal foundations alone but rather...by the relationship it establishes between "practices and speculations," or between techniques and doctrines.[12]

Pregadio's insight that the laboratory of the Great Work always operated on mystical religious foundations of varied content and origin is illustrated by the texts of Greco-Egyptian alchemical tradition. Zosimos of Panopolis, a Greek speaking Egyptian who flourished around 300 A.D., is the earliest alchemical writer to have had a large enough portion of his work survive to afford a full-fledged scholarly examination and analysis. Zosimos believed that alchemical operations were to be conducted at propitious times and seasons, taking into account various astrological and meteorological factors. Indeed, Zosimos's astrology is that of Egypt, with its Babylonian provenance, adapted Zodiac, and openness to Judeo-Christian and even Gnostic articulations.[13] Not only that, but Zosimos believed in demons, and he used the same terms for God that are found both in certain Gnostic writings as well

---

12. Fabrizio Pregadio, *Great Clarity: Daoism and Alchemy in Early Medieval China* (Stanford, CA: Stanford University Press, 2006), 23-24. Interior citation Robert Halleux, *Les texts alchemiques* (Turnhout: Brepols, 1979), 49.
13. See Jack Lindsay, *Origins of Astrology* (New York: Barnes and Noble, 1971).

as in some Neoplatonic treatises. Another name that pops up in Zosimos's work is "Hermes," who Zosimos cites from the influential *Corpus Hermeticum*, that body of texts whose idiosyncratic spiritual teachings inspired the coining of the term Hermetism, or Hermeticism. So, how do we get a grasp of this thing called alchemy? And, while we are at it, why have we not mentioned gold? Alchemy *is* gold-making, right?

The Sacred Art of Alchemy: Mystery, Not Myth

In the Egypt of his time, Zosimos was a master craftsman and a religious guide of the highest order. Indeed, he was a trainer of trainers in the world of Egyptian craftsmen, as we can ascertain from his writings. Zosimos cites Democritus's *Physika* often, and he doubtless follows Democritus in seeing the true alchemical teaching not as a mere myth, but as a "mystery."[14] In the Hellenistic world, "mystery" or "mysteries," at least in the context Democritus used it, referred to initiatory rites and pieties that constituted a spiritual journey for the initiate. Over the course of this journey, the traveler underwent purifications (which may have include fasting and bodily privations), heard sacred words chanted or read to him or her, and who finally viewed certain sacred objects. The end result, for the initiate, was 1) immediate (and possibly ecstatic) communion with the cult deity, and 2) a guarantee of safe conduct to the Isles of the Blessed or to the heaven beyond the realm of the fixed stars.[15]

The foregoing brief discussion of Zosimos's background—with its ties to Hermeticism, Egyptian temple worship, and mystery cults—gives us a suitable starting point for understanding where alchemy came from; indeed, it is quite a different picture than that painted in the lurid though gripping tall tales of Medieval romances. The Medieval period had its castles, its knights, and its jousting tournaments, all of which have been painlessly transferred (though not without inevitable distortions) to Walter Scott's mega-selling historical novels and to Hollywood

14. Berthelot, *CAAG* 2.1.
15. Wilson, *Iōsis*, 7.

movies such as *Robin Hood*. Umberto Eco's *The Name of the Rose*, despite its unconventional setting—a Medieval *monastery*, no less!—succeeded both as a novel and a motion picture. By contrast, the period between the height of Augustan Rome and the dawn of the Middle Ages at the beginning of the 6th century—called Late Antiquity in the scholarly world—offers few conceptual landmarks or iconic scenes to correspond to the Medieval period's seemingly built-in melodrama.

In fact, it has taken the rare gifts of such erudite scholars as Averil Cameron and Peter Brown to provide anything approaching a reliable roadmap to the social and intellectual life of Late Antiquity. The enigmatic haze that is the political and economic history of the period is quite enough to provoke fits of clothes-rending, but any attempt to trace the *general* thought patterns of Late Antique man—that is, to find the commonalities between its socio-political and religious aspects—seems to require even more patience. The biggest problem—and this complaint applies especially to the corpus of alchemical writings from the time—is the casual and vague manner in which writers of the epoch borrow and adapt teachings and sayings from a wide array of textual and cultic traditions, often subtly altering these nodes of information and doctrine in accordance with their own difficult-to-determine aims and worldviews.

Amidst all of this ambiguity and uncertainty, I argue that there does seem to be a "theory" of alchemy that we can isolate, though it must be stipulated from the get-go that this theory has many varieties, in the same way that Platonism, despite its myriad incarnations, retains certain unmistakable features or motifs that ring out differently depending on the historical period in which they are played. For those who are suspicious of the kind of sweeping history that imposes an imagined unity on totally disparate historical events, let it be known that I do not plan to go beyond widely accepted facts about history and the diffusion of cultures, although this "wide" acceptance is often hidden in various studies spanning different languages and disciplines, and thus needs to be drawn together, as indeed this study hopes to do. Alchemy meant many different things to many different people, but because so many alchemical writings speak about reducing metals to a primal state and also about snakes biting their own tails and World Eggs, I feel more than warranted in theorizing about what these identities, far-flung over vast stretches of space and time, *mean*.

So, suffice to say the following pages will include a generalized overview of how early alchemists described the actual process of transmutation. I will choose features, themes, and operations that are spoken of by alchemists from different times, places and groups. Before attempting this overview of the actual alchemical process(es), however, we will first discuss ancient Greek matter theory and how it developed into Pythagorean cosmic teachings. Without this context, the subsequent discussion of alchemical process would be incomprehensible.

Prima Materia

In the first century B.C. we find new types of heating vessels referred to and even depicted in Greco-Egyptian documents. One such vessel was the *kerotakis*, represented right.

At the bottom of the cylinder was a wood or charcoal flame that heated a mass of mercury or sulphur located on a platform partway up the furnace, the whole apparatus being closed rather than open to the air. Fumes from the heated mercury or sulphur rose up through the holes in a metal plate that lay flat across the lip of the cylinder. Over the metal lid was placed a bowl, and within the upper chamber was put a chunk of silver or some other ore with precious metals hidden within. The result of this metal cooking operation is interesting: *First the mercury or sulphur fumes cause the ore above to blacken with oxide, then to turn white as the mercury accumulates on the metal's sur-*

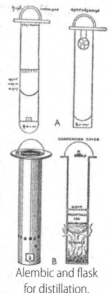

Alembic and flask for distillation.

face, and finally, as a third stage in the transformation, the ore turns yellow as the gold and/or silver in the chunk bonds with the particles of mercury on the metal's surface. If we follow A.J. Hopkins in focusing on the indirect path taken by the sulphur fumes (the direct path being the heating of the ore by the fumes through the grate-holes), we observe another process, parallel to the ore mass's color changes, that adds another dimension to the spectacle: The rising fumes of sulphur pass through the holes in the *kerotakis* plate and condense on the cooler head at the top of the cylinder; then, the condensed drops fall down upon the mass of ore that sits on the central sieve, this being referred to as the metal's "bath" by alchemical texts, since the drops are "constantly bathing the shiny alloy causing it to lose its metallic sheen and changing it to a black sulphide." Thus, the sulphur/mercury "pursues" the metal through "aer" and through water, an odd fact that surely was not lost on the alchemist, who was already aware of the idiosyncratic properties of mercury and sulphur.[16]

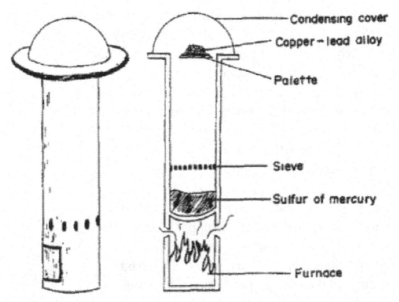

Modern drawing of a kerotakis vessel with labeled parts.

Condensing cover
Copper – lead alloy
Palette
Sieve
Sulfur of mercury
Furnace

---

16. A.J. Hopkins, "A Study of the Kerotakis Process as Given by Zosimus and Later Alchemical Writers," *Isis* 29.2 (November, 1938): 326-354, at 329-330.

Though this process does not create gold, it does create an alloy that is gold in hue. This is the process (or at least one of the processes) that inspired alchemists to theorize about what they were accomplishing and how they were accomplishing it. Since this earliest alchemical transmutation was actually a specific type of metal tinting, we may conclude that, to these Greco-Egyptian alchemists at least, changes of color indicated changes of nature, of *physis*. *To the alchemists, the different colors—black, silver, gold—indicated different levels or modes of existence (both for the metal and for themselves), these levels, in turn, correspond to different regions of the cosmos.* Gold corresponded with 1) the sun, as well as 2) aither (fiery air) in particular, and with 3) the highest region of the universe in general, the latter being beyond the realm of the fixed stars in some writers' conceptions. This idea of a metal-heaven nexus goes back to ancient man's original discovery of metal in meteorites. To judge by ancient and modern evidence of folk practice and belief, the metal that fell to earth in meteors was originally believed to have been broken-off fragments of the substance of heaven! Evidence reveals that a similar belief was—and in some places, still is—held about natural crystals. Because of the geometric regularity of their shapes and their often bright hues, it was believed by many that natural crystals were fragments of hardened fire—this fire conceived as a kind of spark or energy of the cosmos—owing perhaps, paradoxically, to their apparent greater level of abstraction compared to other mineral fragments. Indeed, these precious gems and crystals appeared not unlike basic building blocks of more differentiated bodies; as substances existing in a state closer to the undifferentiated primal waters of creation, they were honored as celestial substances made of a more perfected stuff. (Also note that this craft-folk belief about natural crystals seems to be the inspiration for Plato's idea of the progression of five regular solids.)[17] Later, Babylonian astronomy added the idea that

17. See Sir William Ridgeway, "What Led Pythagoras to the Doctrine that the World Was built of Numbers?," *Classical Review* 10.2 (March, 1896): 92-95, wherein Sir William points to Pythagoras's training as a gem engraver as an influence

a number of regions surrounded the earth like concentric circles, each one purer and closer to perfection than the one it encased; also from Babylon comes the idea of the twelve sections of the sky corresponding to a god—the Zodiac.[18] As for the concentric spheres, each was ruled by an archon, and each archon was associated with a metal, the scale of metals moving from base metals like tin and lead up to, at the highest reaches of the heavens, silver and gold. By the time we arrive at the first centuries A.D., the early alchemists in Hellenized Egypt such as Democritus, Mary the Jewess and Zosimos of Panopolis have dovetailed all of these strands with Greco-Egyptian spiritual practices to create what they called the Great Art, though it is doubtful that they thought themselves to be "creating" anything, alchemy being seen as a kind of divine gnosis that reveals, not merely some aspects or types of process, but rather *reveals the reality and power of process itself.* Part 1 will explore the most salient orientations that tie in to this cosmic power flow, namely the spiritual, cosmic and theological.

At this point, we must come to grips with an element that is central to any notion of alchemy, but about which we have thus far merely hinted: Hermetic cosmology. What is meant by "Hermetic"? Well, the actual term Hermetic indicates anything originating from or inspired by Hermes Trismegistus ("Hermes the Three-Times Holy"), a mythical being who was thought by many to have initiated all magical and/or mystical traditions (see *Glossary* entry "Hermeticism"), including alchemy. For our purposes, I am using the adjective Hermetic to mean any text or artifact that relates to that stripe of Hellenistic religion that includes some or all of the following characteristics:

---

on his probable belief that natural crystals are from the pure realm of the heavens, a belief reflected in Plato's comment in the *Phaedo* that precious stones such as "sards and jaspers and smaragdi" are pieces broken off of their more perfect forms (Phaedo 63.59.109ff [cited Ridgeway, 93], here conceived in shockingly material terms, at least in comparison with Plato's other teachings about the realm of forms and their immateriality!).

18. Lindsay, *Origins of Alchemy*, 34-35.

1. An emphasis on individual salvation as a safe passage through cosmic spheres that stand between the terrestrial and the heavenly realms.

2. A belief (shared by those called "Orphics") that the cosmos is an organism dual at its very heart, this duality forming not a simple opposition but rather having two complimentary sides—as in an egg's having an inner aspect, perhaps its golden yolk, and an outer aspect, for instance its white or its shell.

3. *These two sides of the cosmic coin and their interrelation*, when viewed from an enlightened perspective, *reveal the deepest nature of all processes*, the secret of controlling the development of individual natures or existents toward perfection. Often this dual-cored cosmos is described in terms of a central point—a limit—that appears in the midst of the undifferentiated and unbounded initial unity. In Orphic texts, this central point is a kernel that emerges from the primal waters, spreads out in every direction from the central node, and finally splits to reveal Phanes, the god of light and father of the other gods. This latter development results in a macrocosm, a World Egg, whose substance partakes of both the "inner and "outer," of light and dark, and whose ambiguous status is overcome by individual beings becoming reunited with their origin, the central light.[19]

4. Perfection is the goal of all existent beings, and that same perfection is the goal of the cosmos as a whole.

Doubtless there are more characteristics we could add to the list, but we will be better served to look at some alchemical texts to flesh out this notion of a Hermetic cosmology.

In "The Visions of Zosimos," a Greco-Egyptian text from around the year 300 A.D., Zosimos of Panopolis purports to pass on the true method and meaning of alchemy by describ-

---

19. This summary of Orphic cosmology is mostly a paraphrase of Wilson, *lōsis*, 6. On Orphism, see entry below in the Glossary and cf. W.K.C. Guthrie, *Orpheus and Greek Religion*, 2nd ed. (London: Methuen, 1952).

ing to the reader a series of dreams. Each dream is presented by Zosimos as an allegory of a particular stage in the transmutation process. For Zosimos, though there are many "colors" or substances utilized in the Sacred Art, "the separation of the spirit from the body, and the fixation of the spirit on the body are not due to foreign natures, but to one single nature reacting on itself, a single species, such as the hard bodies of metals and the moist juices of plants."[20] *First the metallic body is de-spirited; then, and only then, spirit and body are reunited at a higher level of integration and power.* Keep this "giving up the ghost and getting it back" theme (my phrase) in mind while we also bring into focus the Hermetic cosmology, in which the master binary of inner-outer corresponds not only to the Zosimosian spirit-body opposition, but also to other related pairs spoken of in alchemical theory, such as male-female and even good-bad.[21]

Another place in the "Visions" gives us a further initiatory shortcut into alchemical imagery with its Hermetic associations:

> For all things are interwoven and separate afresh, and all things are mingled and all things combine, all things are mixed and all unmixed, all things are moistened and all things dried and all things flower and blossom in the altar shaped like a bowl. For each, it is by method, *by measure and weight of the 4 elements*, that the interlacing and dissociation of all is accomplished.[22]

Zosimos sees the Sacred Art of alchemy and its ascending path from lead to gold as a rise through the realms of the four elements—earth, water, air, and fire. In this, he seems to be following Plato's cycle of the elements presented in *Timaeus*. In order to grasp the significance of this alchemical ascension through the four elements, we must circle back to the first text

---

20. Zosimos of Panopolis, "The Visions of Zosimos," trans. F. Sherwood Taylor, *Ambix* 1 (1937): 88-92, at 88.
21. Below we will explore the intricacies of this philosophical and mystical notion of a "Table of Opposites," which Aristotle and other ancient writers claimed were core doctrines of the Pythagoreans. For this Pythagorean system of binaries, see Aristotle, *Metaphysics* A5, 986a 24-6; and idem, *Physics* 3.2, 201b25-27.
22. "Visions of Zosimos," 90. Emphasis added.

we mentioned, Democritus's *Physika kai Mystika*, which contains—if we are to judge by the frequency that it is cited by other prominent alchemists—undoubtedly the most important passage from any alchemical work, period:

> "One nature delights in another nature; one nature conquers another nature; one nature over-rules another nature" (c. 3; trans. Wilson, *Iōsis*, 3).

C. Anne Wilson made the astounding discovery that the Greek verbs used in this passage—forms of *nikēthen* and *karatēthen*— were taken from Plato's *Timaeus* 58d, where the Athenian was presenting Pythagorean views about the cycle of the four elements' transformations.[23] This is significant because the most revered symbol of the Pythagoreans was the tetraktys, pictured below.

The tetraktys was the symbol used by the Pythagoreans to illustrate the cosmic path to perfection.

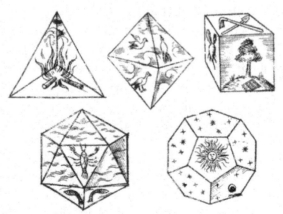

A modern depiction of Plato's five regular solids.

23. C. Anne Wilson, "Pythagorean Theory and Dionysian Practice: The Cultic and Practical Background To Chemical Experimentation in Hellenistic Egypt," *Ambix* 45.1 (March 1998): 14-33, at 18.

The oath that the Pythagoreans swore over this symbol stated that the tetraktys represented "the fountain and roots of overflowing nature."[24] For the followers of Pythagoras, the bottom row of four points represented earth, the row of three was water, two was air or aither, and one was fire. The starting point for this tetraktys cosmology was the opposition between heaven and earth, the 1 and 4 of the tetraktys. Air and water were seen as the two mediating terms, sharing qualities with both fire and earth. In fact, the process of elemental change as presented in the *Timaeus* shows a marked ambiguity toward earth in that the other three elements are composed of tetra-hedra whose surfaces constitute 3-4-5 "perfect" triangles (in what is here called the perfect triangle, the hypotenuse is twice the length of the shorter leg), which cannot be changed into earth, the latter being the only element made up of cubes that can be divided into pyramids with scalene triangle surfaces that cannot be changed into the 3-4-5 pyramids that make up water, air, and fire.

However, this idea of earth as the odd element out does not hold if we observe the actual elemental cycle and its metallic aspect as put forth by Plato's text. The *Timaeus* names cop-per, the earthy metal containing gold seeds (which seeds are kernels of solidified aitherial fire) as the starting point in the process that ends in a transformation of all the elements into the "1" at the top of the tetraktys. C. Anne Wilson is worth citing at length here, since her speculative reconstruction of the Pythagorean-alchemical theory of transmutation comple-ments nicely our earlier tentative sketch of what must have been going in the first alchemical labs in Egypt:

> Copper represented *earth on its way to becoming water.* The people who compiled the chemical recipes knew how to obtain mercury and arsenic from their sulphides by vaporization processes which demonstrated that a gaseous or airy nature was concealed within the sul-phide. They heated their copper *petalon* with mercury

---

24. Aetius, *De placitis philosophorum*, 1.3.8. Cited in Wilson, *Iōsis*, 17, endnote at 99.

or arsenic in a sublimation vessel, and it emerged with *a silvery appearance, thus representing water on its way to becoming air.* It was then tinted gold by means of sulphur, sulphur water, yellow minerals and plant dyes in various combinations, and at this point may have represented *air on its way to becoming fire*, but not yet fully fire.... (-) Further treatment...brought the copper to its final gold state when the element fire became its predominant "nature."[25]

Here the earth-and-metal copper is brought to a watery, soul-rich state via the sublimation process, wherein the airy, aitherial fumes from mercury and sulphur first blacken the copper, then whiten it, making the latter a fit receptacle (being pure and virgin, an ivory *tabula rasa*) for the fiery color that evinces its passage into immutability, for, as one Vedic text has it, "gold is immortality and fire is immortality."[26] The resultant metal, gold, as incarnated fire and stabilized immutability, is aptly compared to the essence of the divine. Humble copper, in the final analysis, turns out to be the necessary counterpart to the fiery "1," the lowly earth—the cold and dark womb, Gaia—possessing the necessary female alter-energy that gives the fiery male energy a space around which to coil and thus to develop its energies. In other words, the vision of aurification presented in the *Timaeus* that is taken over and adapted in the first alchemical text—Democritus' *Physika kai Mystika*—is founded upon an explicitly Pythagorean/Orphic cosmology, symbolized by the most holy sign of the Pythagoreans, the tetraktys.

The *Physika*'s key proverb—repeated incessantly in alchemical texts from the Leyden papyrus to Mary the Jewess and later Stephanos, Geber, and later European writers—speaks of natures first rejoicing in natures, then of natures conquering natures, and lastly, of natures prevailing over natures; this formula

---

25. Wilson, "Pythagorean Theory," 18. Emphases added.
26. *Yajr Veda* 7.4.1.10. Cited in David Gordon White, *The Alchemical Body: Siddha Traditions in Medieval India* (Chicago and London: University of Chicago Press, 1996), 13.

seems to outline the ascent of the lowest form of fire within earth through the watery grave of melted copper ore by the power of the aither ("fiery air") that burns away all imperfections, changing all of the lower natures—the bottom three tiers of the tetraktys: earth, water, and air—to the One that is all.[27]

Heavenly Hades: The Black Sun Theme in Alchemy and Greek Philosophy

Before taking a closer look at some of the inheritors of the alchemical tradition of Zosimos and Democritus, it behooves us to first describe a master theme of Alexandrian alchemy that is also of utmost importance to a wide assortment of coeval mystical groups, be they Pythagoreans, Orphics, or even Gnostics. This alchemico-hermetic theme we will name, following C. Anne Wilson, "heavenly Hades."[28] We have to put aside our Christian preconceptions about heaven and hell for a moment to wrap our minds around this idea. What we have termed the "heavenly Hades" involves a view of the cosmos as a theatre wherein created beings can find their true destinies by becoming united to the ever-present fiery element—the fire of Hades—that is itself divine and which is best defined as a fecund, energy-rich substance where opposing forces—as in the Pythagorean "Table of Opposites"—meet. The seeker who taps into this divine fire can see beyond his immediate physical and mental horizon, and can make soul journeys to spiritual realms, even attaining to unmediated communion with the divine.

Before going beyond this vignette to give a fuller picture of this alchemical idea of a divine Hades, I think it best to pause a moment to lay out a certain difficulty that, if not faced now, will rear its head later, and cause confusions and uncertainties that will be well nigh impossible to dispel. In my studies of

---

27. For a discussion of the "Nature conquers nature" theme in alchemy (including a few citations from later writers), see Paul Plass, "A Greek Alchemical Formula," *Ambix* 29.2 (July 1982): 69-73.
28. Wilson, *Iōsis*, 7.

the texts of Western intellectual and religious history, I have found it rough going at times to determine the attitudes toward matter reflected there. Ever since, as a young man, I first read Arthur O. Lovejoy's *The Great Chain of Being*, a book that contrasts Plato's supposed "otherworldliness" with Aristotle's purported "this-worldliness," I have been dissatisfied with easy schematizations that paper over the ambiguities in this area, though I certainly understand that these schematics are necessary, and that there is much profit in Lovejoy's work. Indeed, I would be quite the philistine to think otherwise.

Illustrative of the haze that surrounds this issue of whether or not Western philosophy sees the material world in a positive or negative light is a discussion I once had with a friend about Plotinus's attitude toward matter. I castigated the author of the *Enneads* for his flight "from the alone to the Alone," which, for me, indicated a devaluation of the world. My interlocutor responded that Plotinus's attitude is not so one-sided, but rather is best understood as a holding together of two opposed perspectives in mind simultaneously: 1) From the perspective of the One, matter is a dark sink that is infinitely distant from the divine, and thus is approached as inferior and even filthy; however, 2) from the point of view of the material realm *per sé*, matter is as perfect as it can be considering its ontological status as a kind of gauzy reflection of the divine.

Indeed, my Socratean friend intoned, the material world is a result of the glowing vessel of the godhead overflowing itself because of its goodness. If the springing up of the final and furthest-out ring—matter—constitutes the first appearance of evil, this does not mean that matter itself is evil through and through. The ambiguity only grows when we consider that Plotinus, in the second *Ennead*, Book 9, rails against the Gnostics and their condemnation of the world and its matter as purely evil. In Part One I offer a more plainspoken critique of a broadly-conceived "Hellenistic anthropology," which of course has a concomitant cosmology. However, for our present purposes it is more fruitful to get inside the heads of the philosophers and alchemists who claimed to view matter as holy (since it originated in the divine), but who also spoke often of shedding the fetid husk of the body and the world it inhabits. That being said, I have to give a caveat concerning the idea of a divine Hades as it is presented in scholar Peter Kingsley's writings (Kingsley's work will be examined in detail below, with citations). According to Kingsley, Plato focuses on a purely immaterial realm that excludes the goodness of nature, and Aristotle reduces man's inner life to a rationalistic faculty, denying the spiritual reality behind the world of appearances. Opposed to the dualism of Plato and the reductionism of Aristotle, in Kingsley's mind, is the mystical monism of Parmenides and Empedocles. Without going into a protracted discussion, suffice to say that Kingsley retains what (at least to this writer) appears to be an ambiguous attitude to matter, though for Kingsley and others who share his mystical conceptions, *this paradox is the whole point.* For instance, Kingsley, in unpublished lectures, has stated that the world is an illusion and that the only reason we have bodies is to be able to move around and communicate with other beings, this function being necessary only because of this alien impediment called the world of space and time. However, at these same seminars, Kingsley scoffs at other mystics who seem to neglect the body in their conceptions of spiritual practice.

Doubtless influenced by a fragment of Empedocles that seems to enjoin the seeker of wisdom to trust each of the senses equally and to strive to perceive the actual mode in which each perception is recorded in our minds.[29] Kingsley advocates a kind of ascetical regimen that includes touching parts of one's body (the specific example of which I am thinking is his suggestion, at a seminar, that those in the audience press their fin-

---

29. "But come, observe with every device in the way in which each thing is clear:
       neither hold sight in more trust than hearing,
       nor resounding hearing above the clarities of the tongue,
       nor let any of the other limbs by which there is a passage for thinking
       be deprived of trust, but think in the way in which each thing is clear"
(Empedocles, B3; trans. Jonathan Barnes in *Early Greek Philosophy*, 2nd rev. ed. [London: Penguin, 2001], 118-119).

gertips on their legs and buttocks and to create a kind of loop in the mind that turns back on the process of perception itself) and also involves solitary meditation of a particular stripe. An active effort to mentally trace the single process of perception as it flows through multiple senses is supposed to lead the seeker to distrust the senses as guides to truth but to simultaneously *use* the *process* of sensation to go beyond the individual percepts to the cosmic flow behind both matter and temporality.

As I hope this brief excursus shows, there are many problems with Kingsley's division of ancient Greek philosophy into the mystical monists on one hand and everybody else on the other. But all of this is illustrative, for what we have in Kingsley is what we will see in much Hellenistic religious discourse: an emphasis upon process at the expense of exclusionary interpretations of categories such as person ("I am the person James and you are the person Roger") and nature (*physis*; "The world's *physis* is created, but the divine *physis* is uncreated"). What I have termed "exclusionary interpretation of categories" is held not only by Orthodox Christians and some non-Orthodox Christians, but is also held to (though in a radically different context than in Christianity) by some Manicheans and Muslims, and by others. Part 1 will spend time refining and developing the notions of process and category as they are evinced in alchemical texts, and fruitful comparisons will be made with Orthodox Christian views of the same themes. There are three main reasons Orthodox Christianity will be used in these pages as a foil to alchemy: 1) Orthodox Christianity existed as a widespread and dominant intellectual and religious paradigm throughout late antiquity; 2) the defining traits of alchemical thinking each have a matching countertrait in Orthodoxy; and, further, 3) I am particularly qualified to speak about the early history of Orthodoxy since I have done extensive research on the subject.[30]

---

30. The question of the relationship of alchemy to the Eastern Roman Empire and its Orthodox Civilization is a tangled one. There is not a large enough sample size of texts from the Eastern Roman Empire that deal with alchemy to draw any meaningful conclusions. In the *Suda* it is written that "Diocletian, having sought out the books on this subject, burned them. Now, because of the revolu-

*** *** ***

When someone asked [Thales] which came first, night or
day, he answered, "Night came first—by day."
                              —Thales of Miletus (ca. 625 – ca. 545)[31]

Any discussion of the "heavenly Hades" cosmology has to
contend with Peter Kingsley's *Ancient Philosophy, Mystery, and Magic*, which irritated many in the academic community when it was published by Oxford's Clarendon Press in 1995, an example being Jonathan Barnes' entertaining but bizarre review, which concluded that Kingsley was a "roaring boy," who "thumps his tub," and "buckles his swash."[32] All of this perhaps indicates Kingsley's headlong plunge into an idiosyncratic, mystical view of the history of Western philosophy. Kingsley gave detailed support for his thesis that Empedocles' and Parmenides' cosmology contrasts starkly with that of the supposed founders of Western thought—Plato, Aristotle and their followers. Before Kingley's book, most scholars believed that Empedocles and Parmenides (both 5th cen. B.C.) were more rationalistic than mystical in their thinking, the latter philosopher being touted as the "founder of logic" (which he

---

tions, Diocletian treated the Egyptians harshly and cruelly and having sought out these books written by their forefathers on the chemistry of gold and silver, burned them lest wealth should accrue to the Egyptians through this art and lest they, emboldened by riches, should in the future revolt against the Romans" (Cited in Grimes, *Zosimus*, 43). As anyone can ascertain, this passage tells us nothing decisive about Diocletian's beliefs about or attitudes toward alchemy, since fiscal control would be a sufficient cause of this Imperial ban. Cf. Michèle Mertens, "Graeco-Egyptian Alchemy in Byzantium," avail. online at: http://orbi. ulg.ac.be/bitstream/2268/14188/1/205-230%20M.%20Mertens1.pdf, for a general picture of the place of alchemy in Eastern Roman society in the time of Zosimos up to that of John Kanaboutzees in the first half of the fifteenth century.
31. Diogenes Laertius, *Lives of Eminent Philosophers*, 1.36, in Barnes, *Early Greek Philosophy*, 16.
32. Johathan Barnes, "(Review of) Peter Kingsley, *Ancient Philosophy, Mystery and Magic*," *International Journal of the Classical Tradition* 4.3 (Winter, 1998): 460-462, at 462. For a piece that illuminates Kingsley's character and which includes Kingsley's recounting of a run-in with an incensed academic at UCLA, see Jeff Munnis, "Peter Kingsley and the Discomfort of Wisdom," *AntiMatters* 1.2 (2007): 143-153.

certainly is, though the significance given to the word "logic" in ancient texts is far from straightforward).

But the heart of Empedocles' philosophy, so Kingsley holds, is a rather Orphic belief that a central fire blazes at the earth's core, a fire intent on making its way to the border of the cosmos, far above the Earth's surface. Fire interacts with the subterranean waters and with the dark earth itself, creating hot springs and volcanoes, sites of holy worship since they *literally* are places where the heavenward forces of the cosmic hearth bubble up to the surface, the hearth-fire being the universal catalyst *par excellence*. From the cosmos's fiery point of origin, it is not only streams of bright flame but also quickly hardening clouds of dark mist and earth that burst forth spore-like from the kernel's earthen crust. This "Big Bang" is the cause of the material universe's expansion in all directions from the central golden dot, the fire (with other elements along for the ride in various proportions) stopping when it reached the spherical cosmic border.

Thus Empedocles and his ilk saw the universe both as a great sphere of earth surrounded by aither, stars and sun; and also as a reaching out of fire and fire-bearing beings toward the celestial borders. The sun and stars are pieces of fire that got trapped on the cosmic "glass" that is the outer shell of the World Egg, and the heavens that surround the celestial bodies are regions of glazed or crystallized aither.[33] Humankind originated, according to Empedocles, from Hades, from below the surface of the Earth. The central fire pushed the first humans into the aither above the Earth. Later, when fiery earth and water burst into the atmosphere, a mass of fire—the sun—collected in the sky and thus light was shed upon the dark face of the Earth. (As a sidebar, also note Empedocles' belief that the weight of the sun, which contained a disproportionate amount of fire in a concentrated spot, actually tilted the whole cosmos slightly, and this accounts for the Earth's axial tilt.) To illustrate just how much Empedocles' conception differs from that

33. Peter Kingsley, *Ancient Philosophy, Mystery, and Magic: Empedocles and Pythagorean Tradition* (Oxford: Clarendon Press, 1995), 49.

of the Judeo-Christian tradition (at least, the Judeo-Christian tradition as it is thought of in the West), let us translate the Empedoclean cosmology into Christian terms: God said, "Let there be light in the center of creation, and let this fire of hell burst forth from the cold, dark earth, suffusing all things with its light and heat" (my phrase).

This fiery hearth cosmology contrasts with more dualistic worldviews that see matter, time and space as a result of a fall from grace. The Gnostics and many Neoplatonists held variants of the latter, decidedly otherworldly view, which may have originated (at least in its decisive articulation) in Plato's doctrine of the "forms." The Hellenistic notion of *soma sema*—the body is a tomb—seems to be akin to this dualistic, spirit-over-matter stance. Kingsley makes the assertion, unsettling for many, that this Empedoclean tradition was carried on in Greco-Egyptian alchemy and in its immediate successor, Arabic/Islamic alchemy.

In order to shed more light on this Hermetic view of the universe and its relevance to alchemy, let us examine the "Poimandres," the first text in the *Corpus Hermeticum*, all the while keeping Kingsley's insights in mind.

The "Poimandres" begins with the unnamed narrator's description of a surreal experience he had of a figure of unlimited size who induced in him a kind of mystical trance:

> Once, when thought came to me of the things that are and my thinking soared high and my bodily senses were restrained, like someone heavy with sleep from too much eating or toil of the body, an enormous being completely unbounded in size seemed to appear to me and call my name and say to me: "What do you want to hear and see; what do you want to learn and know from your understanding?"
> "Who are you?" I asked.
> "I am Poimandres," he said, "mind of sovereignty; I know what you want, and I am with you everywhere."[34]

---

34. "<Discourse> of Hermes Trismegistus: Poimandres," in Brian P. Copenhaver, ed., *Hermetica: The Greek Corpus Hermeticum and the Latin Asclepius in a New Eng-*

Next, Poimandres:

> Changed in aspect and suddenly everything opened before me in a moment and I saw a limitless vision, everything become light, serene and joyous, and at the sight I was smitten with love. And a little afterwards there was a darkness showing up below and coming in its turn, fearful and somber, which rolled in tortuous spirals like a snake, as it seemed to me. And this darkness changed into a sort of liquid nature, shaken in an indescribable manner and exhaling a vapour such as comes from fire and producing a sort of noise, an unspeakable groaning. Then there jetted from it a voice of appeal, without articulation, such as I compared with a voice of [fire].[35]

Here I beg the reader to be patient, for I must cite a lengthy passage from Peter Kingsley, whose interpretation of the foregoing parts of the Poimandres casts a sidelight on the alchemico-hermetic tradition in general and the black sun theme in particular:

> ...Poimandres' revelation starts with him undergoing a number of changes in appearance: he turns into light, then the light turns into dark, then the darkness turns into a watery, primal chaos. (-) The light turns into darkness, fire leaps up out of the darkness. Here is no radical dualism: in Greek philosophical terms it is more or less baffling, but what it does correspond to exactly is the fundamental, subtle and often highly ambiguous idea in ancient Egypt of cosmology mirroring the everyday disappearance and reappearance of the sun, with darkness in one sense the opposite of light but in another sense simply its primeval form.[36]

lish Translation with Notes and Introduction (Cambridge: Cambridge University Press, 1992), 1-7, at 1.

35. Trans. of excerpt from "Poimandres" in Lindsay, Origins of Alchemy, 44-45.

36. Peter Kingsley, "Poimandres: The Etymology of the Name and the Origins of the Hermetica," in R. van den Broek and Cis van Heertum, eds., From Poimandres to Jacob Böhme: Gnosis, Hermeticism and the Christian Tradition (Amsterdam, The Netherlands: In de Pelikaan, 2000), 41-76, at 64-65.

First, there is a startling correspondence between the stages of Poimandres' bodily revelation—1) unbounded light, 2) serpentine darkness, and 3) luminous ascent—and the stages of alchemy—1) blackening, 2) whitening, and 3) yellowing. The initial light phase, where "everything became light, serene and joyous," runs parallel to the starting point of alchemy, which presupposes spiritual preparation and enlightenment before any laboratory work commences. Next comes the blackening phase of alchemical operations, counterpart to Poimandres' light-to-dark change, which is presented—in both "Poimandres" and in alchemical texts—as the coiling of a serpent, the resulting circle constituting a space scissioned off from the uncreated (and thus divine!) prime matter, as a passage from the Egyptian *Coffin Texts* has it: "I bent right around myself, I was encircled in my coils, one who made a place for himself in the midst of his coils."[37]

Ouroboros, the tail-biting serpent

The "Poimandres" describes this blackening phase as a liquefaction of the dark matter, the mass being "shaken in an in-

---

37. R.T. Rundle Clark, *Myth and Symbol in Ancient Egypt* (London: Thames and Hudson, 1959), 50. Orig. cit. H.J. Sheppard, "The Ouroboros and the Unity of Matter in Alchemy," *Ambix* 10 (1962): 83-96, at 91.

describable manner and exhaling a vapour such as comes from fire and producing a sort of noise, an unspeakable groaning." This is an obvious use—in a central text of Hermeticism, no less—of the semantic field of alchemy to symbolize the genesis and development of both the soul of man and the cosmos he inhabits, for it is the alchemical furnace that trembles, the moaning "noise" being the purring of steam or other fumes escaping the hermetically sealed alembic.

Next comes the leaping up of the flaming voice, the "voice of appeal, without articulation." This image of the third and final stage as a returning of the fire, not a boundless light as in the first phase, but rather a flame from the depths of the seeker's soul, to the heights of heaven is probably a reference to the ancient teaching about celestial archons. The archons, in a cosmology that is found as early as Babylon and Egypt and which continues straight up to the Gnostics and alchemists of late antiquity, are the gatekeepers of the planetary spheres, and much Gnostic/mystery cult music seems to have been a rehearsal of passwords necessary for the initiate to get past the seven toll-houses on the way to heaven. Interestingly, each archon was associated with a particular 1) musical tone, 2) vowel (one of the seven in Greek), 3) color, and 4) metal. Also, each toll-house being passed, the ascending Gnostic sheds a particular vice or passion associated with it. At the top of the key, the seventh guard post passed, the seeker is totally free of the evil of matter. The flaming voice is a cry because it is a song; it is an appeal because it is a password revealing the seeker's true home in heaven; it is "without articulation" because the pure music of the spheres is noetic [of the intellect], not perceptible by fleshly ears. Gold is the highest thing, the hue of gods' flesh, totally spiritualized life force, since "the fire assimilates all hard and solid objects to subtle and luminous bodies...."[38]

However, there does seem to be a tension here between the Pythagorean and alchemical notion of a black sun, or central hearth—a notion that comes from Orphism as well as from whatever ancient beliefs preceded Orphism—and the idea of heaven

---

38. Iamblichus, Ib. 5.11, cit. Lindsay, *Origins of Alchemy*, 53.

at the top of the sky—a concept that goes back to Babylonian and Egyptian cosmologies, and even further to the previously mentioned idea of a top layer of the sky made of crystallized aither. The ambiguity, I believe, comes from the double meaning of "black sun." On the one hand, black sun seems to describe the "paradox of destructive force being converted into creative power;"[39] that is, the dual aspect of the unitary process of development, operative on the micro and macro levels. On the other hand, it refers to a stage in the divine process, the coiling of the serpent back onto itself, onto its own unlimited essence. It is as if the divine, intentionally or unintentionally, falls into darkness by carving out a vector of space/time and allowing some of the infinite properties that exist potentially in prime matter to manifest themselves. However, we also have a literal central fire, a hearth or One (Gr. *pan*), out of which flows, if we follow Alexander Polyhistor, individual beings made up of the four elements, the latter tetrad composed of limiteds and unlimiteds in some wise or another.[40] (Plato's *Timaeus* may have been an attempt to bring some mathematical order to these somewhat discombobulated proceedings.) Though there is a cycle of elements, the fire heating the subterranean waters, the waters and earth bursting into the air, etc., do all things end up back at the hearth, or do they escape into the highest realm beyond the glazed fire above? If we focus upon the earliest Pythagorean texts, we find the teaching that the central fire is a kind of creator of all things that weaves pieces of the prime matter—the so-called "limiteds" and "unlimiteds"—into harmonies. Confusing the matter is the fact that the hearth or One is itself the first thing created out of prime matter (*Who* created this hearth/One?). What's more, not all the prime matter was used in making the cosmos, just the unlimiteds nearest the heart at the cosmos' creation. The One breathed in, drawing the unlimiteds into a harmonious relation with the limiteds that were lying around. Thus, the ambiguous status of hearth and heaven in Pythagoreanism originated in some idiosyncrasies of the Orphic cosmos. For the Orphics, the hearth at

---

39. Kingsley, *Ancient Philosophy*, 77.
40. Diogenes Laertius, *Vitae Philosophorum*, 8.25.

the center of the cosmos was identified with the outer rim of the sky, the "castle of Zeus."[41] Phanes, the golden boy hatched from the Orphic World Egg, took up residence in the furthest cosmic rim. Where, indeed, is heaven and hell?

Painting in a columbarium near the Villa Pamfilia in Rome. Note the half-black, half-white eggs, symbolic of the Orphic World Egg.

Pythagorean moral teaching advised self-limitation as an active mirroring—on the level of morality and ascesis—of the natural (that is to say, material) harmony that exists at the cosmic and the individual level. Mixed in was an Eastern notion of reincarnation, one that involved certain exceptional persons ascending to a divine realm beyond the material world. This ascent mirrors the path up to the fiery air at the top of the cosmos, farthest from the earth. Perhaps this, for lack of a better term, Hermetic cosmology is best summed up in the words of an actual initiate of the time, a certain Lucius:

> I drew near to the confines of death, treading the very threshold of Proserpine. I was borne through all the elements and returned to earth again. At the dead of night, I saw the sun shining brightly. I approached the gods above and the gods below, and worshiped them face to face.[42]

41. Aristotle, fr. 204, cit. Walter Burkert, *Lore and Science in Ancient Pythagoreanism*, trans. Edwin L. Minar, Jr. (Cambridge, MA: Harvard University Press, 1972), 37.
42. Apuleius, *Metamorphoses* 11.23, in *Hellenistic Religions*, ed. Frederick C. Grant

Tying it all together: The Emerald Table and Later Byzantine Alchemy

"The Emerald Table"

It is true without lies, certain and most true:
That which is below is as that which is above,
And that which is above is as that which is below,
To accomplish the miracle of the one thing.
As all things came from One, through the contemplation of the One,
So all realities arise from this one thing: adaptation.
Its father is the sun, its mother the moon;
The wind carries it in its belly, its nurse is the earth.
It is the father of all perfection throughout the whole world.
Its power is perfect if it is turned into earth.
Thou shalt separate Earth from the Fire,
The subtle from the gross, gently and with great sagacity.
It ascends from Earth to Heaven, then again descends to Earth,
And receives the powers of things above with things below.
Thus thou shalt possess the glory of the whole world,
And all obscurity shall flee from thee.
This is the power of all power,
For it overcomes every subtle thing
and penetrates every solid substance.
Hence proceed wonderful adaptation,
of which the means are here established.
Therefore I am called Hermes Trismegistus,
Having the three parts of the philosophy of the whole world.
That which I had to say regarding
the operation of the sun is completed.[43]

The earliest version of this most famous of alchemical tracts is in Arabic, and may date from the time of the composition of the Koran. Some scholars have recognized that this text probably has a Greek original, and that it may have been composed by al-

---

(Indianapolis and New York: Bobbs-Merrill, 1953), 142.
43. Slightly altered from Gilles Quispel's translation in "Gnosis and Alchemy: The *Tabula Smaragdina*," in van den Broek and van Heertum, *From Poimandres to Jacob Böhme*, 303-333, at 304. For original Latin translation from the Arabic, see George Sarton, "Review of Julius Ruska, *Tabula Smaragdina*," *Isis* 9.2 (June, 1927): 375-377, at 375-376.

chemists in the time of Zosimos. Considering the content of the *Emerald Table*, whose author is unknown, I am at once struck at its emphasis upon "*adaptatione*," or adaptation as the power of all powers. The tale here is not one of heavenly powers that thunder down on a pitiful creation. Rather, creation itself, the process that resulted in all of existence, is available to the alchemist. The method is given in the *Table*, though obscurely so: Harness the fire of the furnace to slowly burn away the earth from the gold, using of course the sulphur/mercury *kerotakis* process which we have described previously. "Its power is perfect if it is turned into earth." Obviously, we are dealing here with an earth that has fire in it, separated from the earth with no fire in it. This may be a reference to the "red sulphur" which became the focus of Islamic alchemy in the seventh century and after.

Also of note is the idea in the *Table* that reality is divided into an upper and a lower level, and that the "power of powers," "adaptation," comes about by the joining up of the upper and lower realms' complementary powers. Here we have the two properties necessary for divine development: 1) uncreatedness, and 2) multi-level self-emanation. The "One" here is perhaps all-powerful, but instead of being locked into "the Alone," the One rather flows outward, like a caged divine Bull giving Itself room to rear. Compare this central alchemical theme to the words of Zosimos:

> This is the divine and great mystery, the object of research, because this is the All. Two natures, (but) only one substance, because one attracts the other and one dominates the other. This is the silvery water, the hermaphrodite, which constantly flees, which hurries toward the proper realities; it is the divine water that all have ignored, whose nature is difficult to conceive. Indeed, it is not a metal, nor a water always in movement, nor a body (solid), because one cannot seize it. It is the universal in all things, because it at once possesses life and spirit, as well as a destructive power. The one who understands it possesses both gold and silver.[44]

---

44. Grimes 60; orig. cit. Mertens.

So, the creative side of things is perhaps easier to grasp than the "destructive" side. What is destroyed in making the "silvery water," which the Table calls a miraculous "earth"? Perhaps it can be understood when relating it to the two qualities that seem to be necessary in the alchemical "gold," 1) liquidity, and 2) fixity. In other words, the substance created by alchemy must both adequately contain power and also transfer this same power to the alchemist as well as to other substances. As Maria the Jewess put it: "If you do not demetalize metals and do not metallize the unmetals and make the two one, nothing expected happens."[45]

As we flash forward to later Byzantine alchemy, specifically the seventh century, we encounter writers such as Stephanos of Alexandria, whose famous lectures on alchemy, which were quoted incessantly by many later practitioners in Arabic and in Latin, included a tetrad of poems from which the following was excerpted:

> By linking soul to body in one bond,
> Th[r]ough perfect combination of the two
> The 'Sacred Art' makes both to live as one,
> When spirit comes a third to crown the whole.
> Exert thy mind in contemplation, first
> Of all philosophy, of secret words
> And intricate ideas of ancient lore.
> Then strive, assisted by thy technic skill,
> (-)
> To know the union of the elements." (17-24, 26)[46]

This passage is as good a segue as any into our first chapter, which will examine more closely this alchemical notion of a mysterious "third" power, a kind of Holy Ghost that works much like Descartes' pituitary gland, playing director, overseeing the Great Work. All good and fine, I concede, but we

---

45. Georgia Irby-Massie and Paul T. Keyser, *Greek Science of the Hellenistic Era: A Sourcebook* (London and New York: Routledge, 2002), 239.
46. C.A. Browne, "Rhetorical and Religious Aspects of Greek Alchemy," *Ambix* 2.3 (December, 1946): 129-137.

all know the problems Cartesius' infamous gland presents. Is it physical or mental, a thing of spirit or a thing of atoms? And those elements, those "roots" that constitute a "few" betwixt the One and Many, what of those?

1

THE
ALCHEMICAL TRINITY

If we ask why, in spite of...openness to different numbers, the number three has prevailed, it seems most probably that the three corresponds to the intrinsic dialectics of experienced life."

–Paul Tillich[1]

The Dao generates the One, the One generates the Two, the Two generate the Three, the Three generate the ten thousand things."

–Daode jing[2]

1. Paul Tillich, *Systematic Theology*, 3 vols. (Chicago: University of Chicago Press, 1963), 293. Cited in David L. Miller, *Three Faces of God: Traces of the Trinity in Literature and Life* (Philadelphia: Fortress Press, 1986), 13.
2. Cited in Fabrizio Pregadio, "Alchemy. China," in *New Dictionary of the History of Ideas*, ed. Maryanne Cline Horowitz, 6 vols. (Detroit: Thompson Gale, 2005), 1.38-40, at 40.

Charlemagne was King of the Franks from 768 and Emperor of the Romans (Imperator Romanorum) from 800 until his death in 814.

Chapter One

The *Magnum Opus* of the Franks: The Carolingian "Shield of Faith" and the Preservation of Cosmic Analogy Triadology in the Western Church.

A t the end of our introduction we found ourselves in seventh century Egypt, where we examined a snippet from the pen of Stephanos of Alexandria. We did not mention, however, that Stephanos dedicated his famed lectures to Heraclius (ca. 575 – 641 A.D.), the Roman Emperor whose ecumenist policies raised the hackles of many in the Church. Heraclius was by all accounts friendly to a wide range of ideas, and was interested in philosophy as well as theology. Stephanos' lectures, besides being written for an imperial figure known for his involvement in theology, also included many references to Christian theology, at one place even asking for the blessings of the Father, Son, and Holy Spirit. Thus, in tracing the forward path of alchemy from its Egyptian beginnings to its arrival in Medieval Europe (by way of Islamic texts in Spain), we are obliged to add another variable to our already crowded equation—Christian theology. But that is far from all. *By the thirteenth century, during which alchemy became widespread in Western Europe, there was a plurality of Christian Churches—1) the Eastern or Greek Orthodox, 2) the Roman Catholic, and 3) the Oriental Orthodox Churches.* Herein lay quite a tale, which, due to space constraints, we must squash into a vignette. Though the Oriental Orthodox Churches (or at least some individual prelates from those Churches) had a

hand in transmitting alchemy to the Arab world (and thus in-
directly to Europe), as many of their theologians and clergy-
men fled to the Far East in the aftermath of the Fourth Ecumenical Council (451 A.D.), bringing their Greco-Egyptian
alchemical knowledge with them.

In the aftermath of the Seventh Ecumenical Council (787
A.D.) of the Christian Church, which promulgated the Orthodox teaching that icons are necessary to Christianity and
must be venerated, we see the Frankish Church under Charlemagne (ca. 742 – 814 A.D.) holding its own national church
council. At this Council of Frankfurt (794 A.D.), Charlemagne
condemned *both* the position of the iconodules (venerators of
icons) *and* that of the iconoclasts (those against icons).

The Franks were that martial Teutonic group who took
over many positions of power in Europe once the Western
Roman Empire became only a memory in the hearts of many
a Gallo-Roman. The Council of Frankfurt has been cited
by many scholars of ecclesiastical history as an example of
Charlemagne's ingenious penchant for geopolitical scheming, his goal being, it seems clear, to keep Rome and the West
separated from the Christian East. Why else condemn both
sides of the icon controversy? The Frankfurt council steered
a middle path by upholding the *use* of icons but also con-
demning their veneration! No matter which side prevailed
on the Eastern front, Charlemagne could then declare the
winning group heretical. All that was needed was *a distinctive theology that could be forced on a weak Pope, and then the
job of divide and conquer was completed.* The trump card was
the *filioque*.

That Charlemagne's goal was to pressure the papacy into
accepting his idiosyncratic "Frankish theology"[3] is evinced by
the controversy that resulted in the early ninth century con-

---

3. I am not aware of any Medieval commentators who used the term "Frankish
theology," but certain aspects of Frankish piety were called "Frankish" by Eastern
Romans in the 13th century and thereafter. I am thinking here of the Greek term
"*frangcopanagia*" (Frankish Virgin Mary) for the rosy-cheeked, Teutonic-styled
icon of the Virgin Mary that the Franks brought with them from the East in the
aftermath of the 4th Crusade (1204 A.D.).

cerning the *filioque* clause that the Franks had added to the Nicene Creed. When the Creed was chanted at the Frankish palace at Aachen, the Holy Spirit was professed to proceed from both the Father *and the Son* (*filioque*). Charlemagne tested the religio-political waters by sending a group of his *filioque*-chanting monks to Jerusalem, where some Greek Christians who happened along were scandalized at hearing the interpolated Creed. A certain John led a kind of Christian commando raid on the Latin monastery. Psalters were confiscated and the *filioque* declared a heresy by the offended Greeks. Shocked Latin monastics (surely with Charlemagne's knowledge) wrote to Pope Leo III. They meekly inquired of the Holy Father: Are the Greeks right in calling us heretics? Pope Leo later declared that it was not proper to change the Nicene Creed, which did not originally contain the Greek equivalent to the Latin "*filioque*," "and the Son." This problem of papal inflexibility was solved when the Franks realized that they could manipulate papal elections behind the scenes. Charlemagne's descendents, following their forefather's stratagem, succeeded in getting the *filioque* officially accepted in Rome by 1009, and even took over the papacy itself during the "time of the German popes" in the middle of the eleventh century.[4] In 1054, the papal representative Cardinal Humbert hurled a bull of excommunication at the Patriarch of Constantinople Michael Kerularius and others besides. This greatest of schisms continues up to today: Orthodoxy in the East and Roman Catholicism in the West.

*** *** ***

In order to come to grips with the subtleties of filioquist theology, we will now take a close look at the famous pictogram known since the Carolingian era as the "Shield of Faith" (fig. 1, page 157). This figure, the earliest examples of which date to just before Charlemage's reign, was intended to express the Christian West's religious faith in the Holy Trinity. It consists of three circles arranged in a triangular pattern, each circle bearing the name of a

4. George Every, *The Byzantine Patriarchate, 451-1204* (London: SPCK, 1962), 107.

Divine Person—Father, Son, and Holy Spirit. In the center of the triangle is a fourth circle, one labeled simply "God."[5]

Most significant for our purposes is the fact that some versions of the "Shield of Faith" place the Holy Spirit at the bottom of the figure, below the horizontally positioned Father and Son, both of whom occupy an upper corner of the top-heavy triangle. This aspect of the diagram is meant to indicate the dual origin of the Holy Spirit, Who, in Western Christianity, is believed to proceed from the Father *and the Son* (*filioque*). Farrell comments: "...[I]t may come as a surprise to many people [that] the doctrine which came to prevail in the mediaeval Latin Church was not the original Christian doctrine of the Trinity, which survived only in the Orthodox Catholic Churches of the East."[6] While it is not our immediate purpose

5. On the "shield of faith," or *Scutum fidei*, see Michael Evans, "An Illustrated Fragment of Peraldus's Summa of Vice: Harleian MS 3244," *Journal of the Warburg and Courtauld Institutes* 45 (1982): 14-68. Significantly, Evans sees the *Scutum fidei* as the visual expression of the Athanasian Creed, which originated around 500 A.D. in Spain, and which is the first historically verified appearance of the *filioque* doctrine (!). Moreover, Evans astutely points out that the *Scutum fidei* was a result of the Mediaeval West's fascination with visual/geometrical figures representing logical principles. In this case, the shield represents the "square of opposition." There could be no clearer evidence of the Mediaeval West's Augustino-Platonic theological method of a dialectic of oppositions than this figure of the Holy Trinity as a divine system of logical oppositions:

> This, like most graphic epitomes, owes more to visual than verbal exegesis. Its source is the diagrammatic logical figure of the square of opposition. The adaptation of scientific diagrams and demonstrations to religious ends was attractive to medieval designers, and the dialectical visual aid in a triangular redaction economically set out the tenets of the Athanasian Creed. The simple addition of a horizontal bar to the limb connecting the terms 'deus' and 'filius' endowed the figure with allusions to the Incarnation and Redemption without diminishing its effectiveness as a demonstration of trinitarian doctrine. (-) The transformation of this simple yet cerebral figure into a shield accords with a tendency for abstract schemata to be realized as objective designs... (Evans, "Peraldus's Summa," 24).

For a more general study of the medieval West's penchant for diagrammatic theological presentation see idem, "The Geometry of the Mind: Scientific Diagrams and Medieval Thought," *Architectural Association Quarterly* 12.4 (1980): 32-55.

6. Farrell, *Philosopher's Stone,* 43.

to argue for or against a particular religious creed, it does behoove us to recognize that the filioquist Trinity was first ratified as dogma in the Christian West by Charlemagne's national church councils in the late eighth and early ninth centuries. Also, we should realize the little known fact that the original Christian Creed—the Nicene-Constantinopolitan—is still proclaimed by the Christian East though not by the Western Churches, who added the words "and the Son," to the original "I believe in the Holy Spirit, who proceedeth from the Father."[7]

Farrell reminds us that this filioquist Trinity is at its core a binity—in other words, there is a "2" hiding behind the "3"—since it places the Holy Spirit on a lower ontological level than that of the Father and the Son. Thus, the Western Trinity is really "two and one," two Persons and their one common energy. Indeed, the Holy Spirit depicted on the "Shield" is a mere pseudo-person, since He (or, more accurately for the filioquist West, *It*) exists merely as the activity of the other two Persons. The Holy Spirit is the "bond of love" between the Father and the Son; *the Spirit is an activity, while the others are fully-fledged Persons who possess their own activity, which activity turns out to be none other than the ghostly Third Person Himself.*

So how does the filioquist Trinity relate to alchemy? Both are based upon what Farrell calls a "dialectic of oppositions," a cast of thought that sees the world as a vast system of binaries, each side of every individual dichotomy being defined by its opposition to its counterpart. The spirit is only spirit because it is opposite to matter, and so on. This dialectical mindset predetermines, in both filioquism and alchemy, that a peculiar line of thought—a specific methodological contour—will be followed. The best way to illustrate the

---

7. Though the Carolingians' engineering of the *filioque* interpolation into the Nicene-Constantinopolitan Creed is well attested, the reader should nonetheless consult the many works of Fr. John S. Romanides, whose researches have shown that is was Blessed Augustine of Hippo's triadological formulation that inspired the Carolingians to base their entire theological edifice on the *filioque*, a fact that proved to be decisive for the Christian West. A good place to start is John S. Romanides, "The Christological Teaching of John of Damascus," *Ekklesiastikos Pharos* 58 (1976): 232-269; and idem, *An Outline of Orthodox Patristic Dogmatics*, trans. G.D. Dragas (Rollinsford, NH: Orthodox Research Institute, 2004).

similarity between the Filioquists' and the alchemists' approach to reality, I am convinced, is to start from the end and work our way backward. In other words, because both groups think alike and are thereby led to the same series of conclusions, we will first list those conclusions. Then, we will flesh out our comparison with a brief examination of relevant historical evidence. First the list of Franco-alchemic "conclusions":

1. God is the radically unknowable monad (Gr. *monas*, unit).

2. However, as the ultimate principle of unity, He cannot fail to imprint the image of His divine unity upon everything that exists in the cosmos[8];

3. God's radical transcendence is conceived in terms of the "dialectic of oppositions," and thus,

4. the *"absolute" separation of the two poles—God and world—is maintained by the (perhaps unwitting) position of a plane of interaction, a middle term which "cuts both ways" in that it can only oppose terms by making them conceptually comparable.*

5. This middle term—this plane of divine-cosmic interaction—promises to keep God and cosmos separate, but ends up defining the unknown term (God) according to the known term (world, and ultimately, man).

6. The result is an *analogia entis*, a theo-cosmological tangent that accomplishes the opposite of its wielder's stated intention.

---

8. Both the filioquist and the alchemical conceptions of God as "monas" resemble the Pythagorean Guillaume Saluste du Bartas'"paradox of the monad," which describes the One as "no Number, but more then a Number yet; / Potentially in all, and all in it" (*His Devine Weekes and Workes*, trans. Joshua Sylvester [Gainesvilles, FL: Scholars' Facsimiles and Reprints, 1965 (1605)], 472. Cited in S.K. Heninger, *Touches of Sweet Harmony: Pythagorean Cosmology and Resaissance Poetics* [San Marino, CA: The Huntington Library, 1974], 85).

Now, with these conclusions in mind, let us now return to that most elusive of texts, the *Corpus Hermeticum*. In the introduction, we sought to demonstrate that the Hermetic writings overlapped, in content and in approach, with Greco-Egyptian alchemy. Here our aim is to show the alchemico-hermetic writings' similarity to the distinctive theological formulations of the post-Charlemagnian West.

*** *** ***

In the *Corpus Hermeticum*, a short exchange between Hermes and his disciple Asclepius is recorded:

> Of what magnitude then must be that Space in which the Kosmos is moved? And what of nature? Must not that Space be far greater, that it may be able to contain the continuous motion of the Kosmos, and that the thing moved may not be cramped through want of room, and cease to move?(— Asclepius): Great indeed must be that Space, Trismegistus(— Hermes): And of what nature must it be, Asclepius? *Must it not be of opposite nature to Kosmos? And of opposite nature to body is the incorporeal...* Space is an object of thought, but not in the same sense that God is, for God is an object of thought primarily to himself, but Space is an object of thought to us,n ot to itself." [9]

The Hermetic trinity presented here—God, Space, Cosmos—has for its middle term "Space" (*topos*). Like St. Augustine's filioquist *Holy Spirit, Who is nothing more than what is common between the Father and the Son* (See St. Augustine, *De Trinitate*, 15.1), the Hermetic *topos* is the tangent between the God Who cannot be conceived and the Cosmos that is God's utter and total opposite. 1) *Space is the soul of the 2) Cosmos-*

9. Joseph P. Farrell, *The Giza Death Star Destroyed* (Kempton, IL: Adventures Unlimited Press, 2005), 239, citing Libellus II: 1-6b, Walter Scott, *Hermetica: The Ancient Greek and Latin Writings Which Contain Religious or Philosophic Teachings Ascribed to Hermes Trismegistus, Vol. 1: Introduction, Texts and Translations* (Boston, MA: Shambhala, 1985 [1924]), 135, 137. Emphasis added.

body, both 1 and 2 being opposed one to another as oil to water. However, the *principle of opposition itself*, viewed from another angle, *becomes a connection between God and Cosmos, for Space as the object of Cosmos' thought is analogous to God as the object of His own thought.* Put differently: Cosmos *becomes* self-conscious through its own soul; God *is* always conscious through his own essence. Man and the World Soul achieve finitely what God is always achieving infinitely.

This seemingly harmless notion of theanthropic analogy is one of the most portentous formulations in the history of religion, for it allows, *mutatis mutandis* [that is, given the appropriate adjustments of terminology], for a Christian mysticism of a beatific vision of God's essence. The God/world/man analogy has not only survived the twists and turns of the Middle Ages and the upheavals of the Modern Era, but in fact thrives as the official theology of the Roman Catholic Church, most recently affirmed at the Second Vatican Council. Some form of *analogia entis* [analogy of being] is also commonly held by other groups of Western Christians.[10]

Herein lay the great significance of the "Shield of Faith" and its alchemico-hermetic basis: The theology of the "Shield" is grounded in the same *analogia entis* that undergirds both the Western theology of beatific vision and the esotericism of the cosmic analogy trinity. *Hermeticism, alchemy, and Western Christianity are in complete accord on this most crucial of dogmas: God possesses in an infinite measure every virtue that man possesses finitely.*

Before delving into a full examination of the iconography of the alchemical trinity in the concluding section of this chapter, we will first outline a few salient features of the Trinitarian theology of the Christian East and compare it to the alchemico-hermetic view.

---

10. Considerations of space prohibit an analysis of the Neo-Orthodox movement in Protestant theology, which ostensibly rejected *analogia entis*, but only by a more trenchant affirmation *analogia fidae*, the belief that the words of Holy Scripture are the sole authority for the Church. See the works by John S. Romanides listed in the bibliography for an analysis and refutation of *analogia fidae*. Fr. John carefully connects *analogia entis* and *analogia fidae* to Augustine, and traces the latter's teachings back to their Hellenistic roots.

Chapter Two

Anthropos, *Cosmos*, and *Theos* According to the Orthodox Catholic Tradition and the Alchemico-Hermetic Tradition: Two Divergent Triadologies.

According to the Orthodox Fathers of the Church, theology's proper beginning point is not any concept of God, however intellectually satisfying or emotionally compelling such an idea may be. Rather, the Orthodox begin with the reality of the Incarnation of Christ, the Son of God. "God became man that man may become as God."[11] The Son is the perfect image of God the Father. We know that the Father, Son and Holy Spirit are three divine Hypostases or Persons because those masters of the spiritual life who have become united to the Holy Trinity in this life all report the same thing: They have become united to the Holy Trinity through a sharing in the divine resplendence or glory (Gr. *doxa*), which, though being from Three, is also One.

However, Orthodox spiritual life has nothing in common with individualism or pietism, for no one can baptize himself, and no one can be perfected apart from the communal life of the Divine Liturgy. One begins as a hearer, as a babe who must begin with milk before he can have solid food. The milk is the opening stages of *ascesis* in the form of 1) obedience to a spiritual father who is a doer, one who teaches from experience of God, and 2) participation in the Holy Sacraments of the Church, the Sacrament *par excellence* being the Holy Eucharist, where the communicant receives the Body and

11. St. Athanasius the Great, *De Incarnatione* 54.

Blood of God into his body. The higher stage that constitutes "solid food" is direct experience of the uncreated glory of God, though the friend of God never rises above the need for repentance and the Sacraments, but rather lives out these aspects of Orthodox life more fully. Such a communion, far from being magical, is in actuality the only Way (Heb. *Torah*) that delivers man from idolatry: "There are two ways, one of life and one of death." "Thou shalt have no other gods before me."[12]

So, if man does not come to know God through concepts, then how does man ever know God at all? Man is created in the image of God, which means that his life is meant to be an eternal journey toward the divine. This journey is possible because man's center is his God-created *nous*, or inner man (*eso anthropon*).[13] The nous is never equated with the brain or the rational mind (*dianoia*) by the Orthodox Fathers; it is precisely this confusion of the noetic with the merely rational that characterizes the Augustino-Platonic tradition of the Christian West. The *nous* is also designated as the heart (*kardia*) by the Orthodox Fathers.[14] This spiritual heart is man's unique organ of communion with the uncreated energies of God. These *energein* of God are not a *part* of God, nor are they an intermediary between man and God. Neither are God's energies anything other than the very Life, Light, and Love of the Father, Son and Holy Spirit. These energies are God's going out of Himself toward creation in an act of love (*kenosis*, self-emptying) to save creation from corruption through communion with His incorrupt life. The recipient of God's energies does not receive a part of God, because God is not composite, but rather man receives the body of Christ, which is a mystico-noetic—and for that very reason eminently

---

12. *"There are two ways"*: The Didache, in *The Ante-Nicene Fathers*, 10 vols., A. Roberts and J. Donaldson, eds. (New York, 1926 [1885-1887]), 1.148. "Thou shalt have no other gods before me": Exodus 20.3.

13. For an excellent introduction to the Orthodox teachings on the nous, see John Chryssavgis, *Ascent To Heaven: The Theology of the Human Person According to Saint John of the Ladder* (Brookline, MA: Holy Cross Orthodox Press, 1989), 70-124.

14. For the identification of the nous and the heart in Orthodox spirituality, see John McGuckin, *Standing in God's Holy Fire: The Byzantine Tradition* (London: Darton, Longman and Todd, 2001), 56ff.

realistic—communication of the life of the Holy Trinity.[15] Nor are the divine energies anhypostatic, but rather are the true resplendence of God, distinguished from the divine essence but not separate from it.

The suffusion of the divine energies throughout all of creation is the overflowing of divine love. *This descent of the Hand of God into the heart of man is the new thing under the sun for which St. Solomon, the prophets, and all of the sages of every era have pined.* God divides Himself undividedly to enter the heart of each and every man who will co-operate with Him to perfect selfless love therein. Accordingly, the true significance of man being "in the image of God" is that man has been created already conformed to God in such a way that he can—with the aid and sustenance of divine grace, that is, synergistically and ascetically—love in the exact way that God loves His creation, that is, freely and selflessly (the only difference being that man is not uncreated by nature, as is the Holy Trinity, but rather man becomes uncreated by grace or energy).[16]

Strictly speaking, only Christ is the Image of God; man is the image of the Image. There is a dual aspect of the image of God in man: Man was created in the image *and likeness* of God. The image of God in man, considered by itself, is a given, for Christ, the Second Adam, through His Incarnation reconstituted the human nature shared by every man. However, the "likeness of God" is not a given, but rather is a task, a Way to be followed, to be lived within. Man transcends himself non-dialectically by emptying himself of all self-concern and *eudaemonia* [well-being] through a co-working with God's uncreated grace, a grace that is not opposed to creation. It bears repeating: God's uncreated glory does not coerce creation into

---

15. See Kelley, *Realism of Glory*, 40-42.

16. The Orthodox teaching about man being created "in" or "according to" the image of God contrasts with the Western Christian view which followed Blessed Augustine's formulation that man is the image of God, a created reflection of God's essence. For a sophisticated discussion of Orthodox and Augustinian "imago Dei" theology see M. Aghiorgoussis (now Met. Maximos of Pittsburgh), "Applications of the Theme 'EIKON THEOU' (Image of God) according to Saint Basil the Great," *Greek Orthodox Theological Review* 21.3 (Fall 1976): 265-288.

acting as a God-serving automaton, but rather ceaselessly calls man (the little cosmos) and all of creation (the big cosmos) into a deeper and deeper union with Him, "from glory to glory."[17] Because the teachings of the Church Fathers are not conditioned by the dubious logic of the "dialectic of oppositions," they can, without any inconsistency, proclaim that God's Hand (his energies) can come down to the heart of man without any resultant development or division in the Godhead. The experience of the Orthodox Fathers of the Church is identical to that of the friends of God of the Old Testament. For example, the Three Holy Children—St. Shadrach, St. Mechach, and St. Abednego—were seen in the fiery furnace with a fourth Person, the Lord of Glory (Christ) who suffered there with them, sustaining them through His grace. Likewise, St. Solomon, standing in the Holy of Holies of the newly-consecrated Temple, marveled that God could at the same time be both beyond and above all of creation, and also come and dwell between the cherubim atop the Ark of the Covenant.[18]

Unlike the Hellenistic/hermetic tradition, which posits an analogy between the life processes of creation and a supposed principle of dialectical development in the essence of God, the Orthodox tradition holds that salvation is *deliverance from the dialectical meanderings of fallen creation*. To state things

---

17. "But we all, with open face beholding as in a glass the glory of the Lord, are changed into the same image from glory to glory, even as by the Spirit of the Lord" (2 Corinthians 3:18). Even though the Orthodox spiritual life is concerned preeminently with experience of God, and even though the Orthodox do not mistake words such as prayers and sacred writings for communion with God in His glory, words are nonetheless central to spiritual life as images or symbols that call the worshipper to communion with God (Gr. *symbollon*: "bringing unlike things together"). It must be stipulated, however, that though the Orthodox proclaim the realism, or reality of God's glory in the heart of His holy ones, they never reify the uncreated, ineffable Light. The danger is that terms like "glory" and "energy," the more they are handled and circumscribed in our reasoning and through our lips, begin to represent God's love as a concept, as something already "known about."

18. Daniel 3.25: "He answered and said, Lo, I see four men loose, walking in the midst of the fire, and they have no hurt; and the form of the fourth is like the Son of God"; I Kings 8.27: "But will God indeed dwell on the earth? behold, the heaven and heaven of heavens cannot contain thee; how much less this house that I have builded?"

starkly, the Orthodox view of man begins with God and views man as an icon of the Godman without any rationalistic analogy being allowed. Orthodox anthropology is thus Hebraic rather than Hellenistic.[19]

In keeping with its Hellenistic basis, the Gnostic anthropology of hermeticism takes man as its starting point: An intuitive feeling—"the call"—provides the Gnostic with an unquestionable certitude that he or she is actually a part of God, albeit a lower emanation of Him.[20] Starting from his human fear of extinction and his desire for self-fulfillment and immortality, the Gnostic projects his eudaemonistic passions into the divine sphere: Man ceases to be a willing subject distinct from other persons and *becomes himself a theo-cosmological process which allows God to know Himself.*[21] Put succinctly, there are three levels in the Gnoseo-hermetic scheme: 1) *Anthropos* (Man), 2) *Cosmos* (World), and 3) *Theos* (God). All three of these levels *are* God, though the first two are lower emanations or manifestations of the divine essence.[22]

---

19. For a discussion of the Hebraic/Hellenistic anthropology from an existentialist viewpoint see William Barrett, *Irrational Man: A Study in Existential Philosophy* (1958; rpt., New York: Anchor Books, 1990), 61-119.

20. On "the call" in Gnosticism see Werner Foerster, *Gnosis: A Selection of Gnostic Texts*, 2 vols., trans. and ed. R. McL. Wilson (Oxford: Clarendon Press, 1972): "The central factor in Gnosis, the 'call', reaches man neither in rational thought nor in an experience which eliminates thought. Man has a special manner of reception in is 'I.' He feels himself 'addressed' and answers the call. He *feels* that he is encountered by something that already lies within him, although admittedly entombed. It is nothing new, but rather the old which only needs to be called to mind it is like a note sounded at a distance, which strikes an echoing chord in his heart" (1.2).

21. John S. Romanides, *The Ancestral Sin*, trans. with an introduction by George S. Gabriel (Ridgewood: Zephyr, 2002). See especially chapter one, entitled "Creation, the Fall, and Salvation in Greek Philosophy in General" (41-49), where Fr. John analyzes the happiness-centeredness of the Hellenistic mind: "The immutable and inactive One of Greek philosophy is rather a projection of the human thirst for a secure understanding of the meaning of existence itself and for *eudaemonia*. It is the object of man's intellectual desire for an entirely natural certainty of salvation but without a real revelation and the gradual saving energy of God in the world. It is also a self-centered principle imaginatively constructed according to the desires of man" (47).

22. For a stimulating discussion of this tripartite gnoseology in the context of the writings of Paracelsus see Elizabeth Ann Ambrose, "*Cosmos, Anthropos*, and *Theos*: Dimensions of the Paracelsian Universe," *Cauda Pavonis* 11.1 (1992): 1-7. For an engaging (but ultimately unconvincing) discussion of gnoseo-hermetic

The foregoing discussion of the Orthodox and hermetic anthropologies is shown to have a great relevance for alchemy if we refocus our attention on the Orthodox and hermetic attitudes toward matter. For the Orthodox, God created the world "very good," and He also created the world in such a way that its material sphere—its matter—is conformable to the incorruption of the noetic realm, the realm of God's uncreated glory. Most importantly, matter is made to be imbued with God's life, not as something foreign to it, but as its own true telos; in this sense, to speak of the alchemical process of changing matter into spirit is inhuman and docetistic,[23] involving the obliteration of creation rather than its deification. With the creation of man, matter and nous/spirit were shown for what they truly are: perfective, non-opposed creations of God which, forever entwined, are intended to ascend from non-defective goodness to greater and greater levels of perfection in God's energies, which energies are His very life.[24] To safeguard the path to union with God and to avoid idolatry and blasphemy, the Orthodox Fathers of the Church distinguished three categories that apply both to the uncreated and to the created:

1) Essence (Gr. *ousia*), which answers the question, "What is it?"

2) Person (Gr. *hypostasis*), which answer the query, "Who is it?"

3) Operation or energy (Gr. *energeia*), which answers the question, "What does it do?"[25]

---

cosmology which strives to contrast a supposedly positive hermetic attitude toward the world with a negative Gnostic view, see R. van den Broek, "Gnosticism and Hermetism in Antiquity: Two Roads to Salvation," in *Gnosis and Hermeticism from Antiquity to Modern Times*, ed. R. van den Broek and Wouter J. Hanegraaff (Albany, NY: State University of New York Press, 1998), 1-20, esp. 9-11.

23. See note 27, pg. 58.

24. Here "*nous*/spirit" refers not to the uncreated energies of God, but rather to the created "spirit of man" which is not a divine "spark" or "piece of God" as the Gnostics would have it.

25. Farrell, *God, History and Dialectic*, 28.

These categories do not stand as analogies of being between God and creation, but instead serve to set the correct boundary between the divine and the created.

By contrast, the Gnoseo-hermetic view holds that the created world is a pale imitation of a truly real realm of Forms. These "ideas" are incorporeal, unchanging and rational. Since an ideal/real oppositional dialectic is presupposed, two superficially distinct cosmological attitudes result: Some gnoseo-hermetic texts denigrate matter as an evil cesspool ruled by demons, while others hold the world to be good. *However, even the seemingly positive Gnostic assessment of the world is just another form of matter-hatred (docetism[26]), since what is held to be "good" in the world is what is hidden within or behind matter.* In other words, matter is a husk, an unreal shadow that contains (or hides) "good" reality.[27] The cellophane wrapper is

---

26. Joseph P. Farrell, in an unpublished typescript in the author's possession entitled "Partial Listing of *Christologies* of Classical Heresies and Gnostics," notes that docetists "begi[n] with the assertion that matter is crude and evil; and so conclud[e] that Christ was pure spirit; the physical appearance was an optical illusion and mere semblance (*dokesis*); Christ was merely God masquerading as man" (4; unnumbered pages).

27. Section two will make apparent why, from a certain point of view, alchemico-hermetic texts seem to praise matter. To anticipate my later argument, matter is "honored" by alchemists because it is believed to have been divided, developed, and "scissioned" from the "aither," the *materia prima*, which is uncreated and which contains every divine attribute. See the Introduction for background on the slightly different context and meaning of "aither" as it was used in Greco-Egyptian alchemy. Titus Burckhardt gives us a sense of the ambiguous, because literally *otherworldly*, attitude toward matter found in alchemy specifically and Hermeticism generally: "In this view, matter remains an aspect or function of God. It is not something separated from spirit, but its necessary complement. *In itself it is no more than the potentiality of taking on form*, and all perceptible objects in it bear the stamp of its active counterpart, the Spirit or Word of God.

"It is only for modern man that matter has become a thing and no longer *the completely passive mirror of the Spirit*" (*Alchemy: Science of the Cosmos, Science of the Soul*, tr. William Stoddart [Louisville, KY: Fons Vitae, 1997], 58-59, emphasis added). Here "ousia" or nature is spirit; matter is reduced to a different ontological category, namely, "function/will/energeia," which lacks a sentient, thelemic existence since everything it *does* is done by someone above who has a nature, that is, who exists and subsists. This ambiguity toward matter seen as the husk containing divine light is reflected in the later American version of hermeticism—American "nature religion"—which denies the reality of the concrete world in order to serve "the world" (Albanese, *Republic of Mind*, 25).

good because one can see through it to the candy it contains. We all know what happens to the wrapper afterwards.

Hopefully the underlying dialectic of oppositions is recognized here, in that motion, matter and unreality is here being opposed to stasis, form and reality. The dualism of this gnoseohermetic view of matter complements the "process dualism" (my term) which lies behind the alchemical trinity. The latter is the yin-yang dualism of "two contrary principles" of which Tenney L. Davis writes, and to which we above alluded. In the following section our examination of alchemical trinitarian imagery will attempt to illustrate how these two dualisms interact in medieval textual illustrations.

Chapter Three

The Archetypal Images of the Alchemico-Hermetic Tradition: Icons of Dialectical Triadology

The Farrellian Definition of Alchemy: Science, Theurgy, and Power

In Taiquing, the earliest tradition of Chinese alchemy, "the central act of the alchemical process consists in causing matter to revert to its state of 'essence' (jing), or *prima materia*."[28] Historically, Indian mysticism, which may have gotten its core transmutational ideas from Chinese alchemy, has sought out ascetic techniques for reversing the cosmological process that caused the differentiation of souls from the original essence, *bráhman*. From the seventh century (and possibly before) we see idiosyncratic forms of alchemical theory and practice in India, though some of its main features indicate a direct dependence upon Chinese alchemical precedent.[29] As we have seen, Greco-Egyptian alchemy's Ouroboros (tail-biting serpent) image represents the paradoxical nature of alchemical transmutation, which is both a return to the undifferentiated liquid of primordial chaos, and at the same time a move forward and upward to an aetherial heaven. Though other notions take center stage from time to time in alchemy's varied history, evidence of the *prima materia* concept is ubiquitous, not just in Greco-Egyptian alchemy, but also in Islamic and European

28. Pregadio, "Alchem.," 38.
29. White, *Alchemical Body*, 19.

alchemy, where transmutation strips matter of its qualities or balances out its elements, humors, or properties.

In an attempt to formulate a typology that applies to each of the types of transmutation listed above, scholar Joseph P. Farrell has written about alchemy as a scientio-theurgic technique of "back engineering" wherein the process of God's emanation of the cosmos from an original uncreated prime material can be reenacted.[30] This human repetition of cosmic creation seems to promise the alchemist the power to do anything to the physical medium that God can do. In other words, *the power to do anything, anywhere is the glittering prize of the Great Work.* The question might here be raised as to why we rarely see claims to such absolute power in alchemical texts. One reason is that alchemy, as a sacred science, in most cases conceives of the would-be alchemist as a holy man or ascetic whose personal humility and worthiness is a prerequisite for any transmutation to occur.[31]

So, the alchemical writings exhibit, not a mere lust for wealth, but rather a search for *prima materia*—the primal, uncreated, undifferentiated embodied matter which can inject a deific transmuting power into material bodies (especially persons).[32] We should not, however, excise the gold out of

30. Farrell, *Philosopher's Stone*, 37.
31. See Vladimir Karpenko, "Alchemy as donum dei," *Hyle—International Journal for Philosophy of Chemistry* 4.1 (1998), avail. online at: http://www.hyle.org/journal/issues/4/karpenk.htm.
32. To see alchemy as nothing more than mercenary magic is just as reductive as Silberer and Jung's unsatisfactory psychological interpretation. See Herbert Silberer, *Hidden Symbolism of Alchemy and the Occult Arts*, trans. Smith Ely Jelliffe (New York: Dover, 1971 [1917]). On the origin of alchemy as iatrochemical therapy which centers upon gold (or earlier, a herbal panacea called soma) as a prime substance imbued with incorruption, see the dozens of remarkable works by S. Mahdihassan listed in Hakim Mohammed Said, ed, *Essays On Science: Felicitation Volume in Honour of Dr. S. Mahdihassan* (Karachi, Pakistan: Hamdard Foundation Press, 1987), 280-309. Also see H.H. Dubs, "The Beginnings of Alchemy," *Isis* 38 (1947): 62-86: cited in Vladimir Karpenko, "From Metals to Human Beings: Medical Aspects of European Alchemy," *Bulletin of the Indian Institute of the History of Medicine* 21.2 (1991): 105-119, at 111. For criticisms of Jung's view of alchemy see S. Mahdihassan, "Alchemy In the Light of Jung's Psychology and of Dualism," *The Pakistan Philosophical Journal* 5 (1962): 95-103; and Walter Pagel, "Jung's Views On Alchemy," *Isis* 39 (1948): 44-48.

the picture, since many alchemists were concerned with producing it, though this aim usually did not exclude the cosmic control notion. It follows logically that alchemy—a specific practice or *way* toward a specific objective—is based upon a specific cosmology, physics, and theology. Farrell's summation of this alchemical worldview is particularly apt:

> ...[A]ll of the existing diversity of the universe stemmed from one underlying "prime matter" or *materia prima*, an absolutely undifferentiated substrate, an "aether" or medium which then began to undergo differentiation. This initial process of "hyper-differentiation" of an undifferentiated medium Schwaller called the "primary scission." Further differentiations are in turn performed upon these initial derivations from the medium, until at last the entire diversity of creation arises. While all this sounds rather fanciful, it is in fact capable of a profoundly sophisticated interpretation from the point of view of certain aspects of modern physics, for an absolutely undifferentiated substrate in fact is physically *nonobservable*; it is therefore, as far as physics is concerned, a *nothing*, even though it may be said that this *materia prima* has some sort of "existence."[33]

Farrell goes on to note that this *materia prima*, as the underlying essence of each and every existent thing, is "*transmutative* in its very nature; it [is], so to speak, a 'pure potential.'"[34] Thus, to do alchemy with either a piece of lead or a solution of mercury and quicksilver, for instance, is to attempt a reconstruction or re-engineering of that object's "'descent' *or process of differentiation from the medium itself*. One had, so to speak, to 'back engineer' the whole process of differentiations."[35]

---

33. Farrell, *Philosopher's Stone*, 36. The "Schwaller" cited is R.A. Schwaller De Lubicz, the noted authority on Egyptian religion and civilization. In his bibliography Farrell includes Schwaller's *Sacred Science: The King of Pharaonic Theocracy* (Rochester, VT: Inner Traditions International, 1988). For a full exposition of Schwaller's interpretation of the Egyptian worldview see Joseph P. Farrell, *The Giza Death Star Destroyed*, 99-129.
34. Farrell, *Philosopher's Stone*, 37.
35. Ibid. The alchemist George Ripley (1415-1490), in the prologue to his "The

Think of Democritus' *Physika kai Mystika* and its idea that
tinting metals transformed their natures, eventually leading to
the transfiguration of matter into the All (to pan).[36]
The implications of the foregoing definition of alchemy are
breathtaking. First and foremost, the Farrellian notion of alchemy as *a practical path to domination of the cosmos through
a transmutation of created material into uncreated material*
provides decisive support for recent alchemy scholarship that
concerns itself with the practical, "laboratory" side of alchemy,
though Farrell's backing-up job is so effective that it ends up
revealing many limitations built into a merely "practical" approach that would leave out the mystical side of things.

In their effort to approach alchemy from the perspective
of a chemical science done in the laboratory, many take as
their prime target C.G. Jung and his followers. Jung believed
that alchemist's real concern—though they may not be fully
conscious of it—was to reach a higher spiritual state, to complete the process Jung calls "individuation." The color changes
the alchemist witnessed in the alembic, Jung believed, corresponded to the alchemist's inner, spiritual changes. In other
words, the alchemist thought he was looking at real changes in
the material in the ambix, but he was really projecting his inner epiphanies and breakthroughs onto the matter in the vessel. This view of alchemy is very popular among mystics who
accept Jung's *a priori* notions of a "collective unconscious" and
"individuation," but they are unconvincing or even incompre-

Compound of Alchemy," describes the process of transmutation in terms which
match Farrell's emphases on 1) reverse engineering of matter and 2) process triadology: "O Unity in the substance, and Trinity in the Godhead.... As thou didst
make all things out of one chaos, so let me be skilled to evolve our microcosm
out of one substance in its three aspects of Magnesia, Sulphur, and Mercury"
(A.E. Waite, ed., *The Hermetic Museum*, 2 vols. [London: J. Elliot and Co., 1893],
2.139. Cited in George B. Kauffman, "The Role of Gold in Alchemy. Part II," *Gold
Bulletin* 18.2 [1985]: 69-78, at 71). F. Pregadio claims that alchemy was viewed as
reverse engineering in early Chinese alchemy. As evidence he reminds us that an
early Chinese term for the philosopher's stone was *huandan*, which means "Reverted Elixir." "...[T]he central act of the alchemical process consists in causing
matter to revert to its state of 'essence' (*jing*), or *prima materia*." In this scheme, to
be transmuted is to be "*huan*," or "reverted" (Pregadio, 38).
36. *Physika kai Mystika*, c. 19, cit. Wilson, *Iōsis*, 3.

hensible to everyone else. One is reminded of Joseph Camp-bell's fascinating studies of world mythology that assume from the get-go that a certain type of hero is found in most or all world myths. These studies amass detail after detail to support their thesis of an archetypal myth, but have come in for devas-tating criticism for ignoring an equally large body of evidence that directly contradicts their pat typologies. Broadly speak-ing, Jung's mystical approach fails to account for alchemical texts' 1) unrelenting focus on nuts-and-bolts chemical opera-tions that are replete with details that cannot be reduced to a mere psychological allegory; and 2) their evidence of alche-mists' unflagging enthusiasm for the Great Work despite con-sistent failure over centuries.[37]

---

37. See above, footnote 33, on Jung's view of alchemy. Our thesis that alchemy is a quest for unlimited power made possible by back-engineering matter does not depend upon the idea of alchemy as an incredibly long history of failure. Farrell is not satisfied with this unlikely prospect, nor is Eric John Holmyard, who recounts a possibly authentic case of transmutation by Johann Friedrich Helve-tius (Johann Friedrich Schweitzer, 1625-1709):

> ...[H]e dropped the pellet [of elixir] into the molten lead: and with-in a quarter of an hour "all the mass of lead was totally transmuted into the best and finest gold."
> When his first amazement was over, Helvetius experienced a recurrence of skepticism, and ran with the gold, while it was yet hot, to a neighbouring goldsmith, who tested it with the touch-stone and declared it to be genuine. The next day all the Hague heard of the marvel, and the Examiner-General of the Dutch Mint, Porelius, asked Helvetius to submit the gold to the thorough ex-amination customary at the Mint. he at once agreed to this sug-gestion, and the gold was thereupon tested, by both quartation and fusion with antimony, by Brectel, a silversmith. The result was a little unexpected, for it was found that the gold had increased in weight by two scruples during the operation; a phenomenon which Helvetius accounts for by assuming that the gold was still "active" and had transmuted into gold two scruples of the silver used in the quartation. The net result of the matter was, he says, that the elixir had converted six drams of lead and two scruples of silver into the purest gold.
> In passing judgment upon this story, it is important to observe (a) that Helvetius was a man of indubitable integrity; (b) that he admits to having been skeptical even up to the last moment; (c) that the account he gives us is almost contemporary, having been published at Amsterdam in 1667; (d) that he prepared the crucible and lead himself; (e) that he and his wife were the only people

We are concerned with Farrell's work because, in some respects, it avoids the two extremes of Jung's mystical approach and some academics' equally wrong-headed notion of alchemy as proto-chemistry devoid of any real religious element. The latter approach is that of Lawrence Principe and William Newman, whose works explain away the mystical language and goals explicitly stated by most alchemists, the goal of their irresponsibly biased approach, it may be supposed, being to cut God and spirituality out of the alchemical picture.[38] How-

present at the experiment; (f) that there is confirmatory evidence of the gold having been tested by Brectel.

On the last point, we have the testimony of Spinoza, who himself paid a visit to Brectel to gain first-hand assurance, afterwards calling on Helvetius, who showed him the gold and the crucible ("Helvetius Meets an Adept," *Aryan Path* 2.10 [October 1931]: 700-703).

For original source see John Friedrich Helvetius, *The Golden Calf Which the World Adores and Desires…* (London: Printed for John Starkey at the Mitre in Fleetstreet near Temple-Bar, 1670). For more on Helvetius, see Eric John Holmyard, *Alchemy* (New York: Courier Dover, 1990 [1957]). For a list of well-documented cases of successful transmutations, see George B. Kauffman, "The Role of Gold in Alchemy. Part III," *Gold Bulletin* 18.3 (1985): 109-119, at 113-114.

38. For example, I follow Walter W. Woodward ("The Alchemy of Alchemy," *The William and Mary Quarterly* 60.4 (2003): 920-924), who decries William Newman's "relegat[ing]…the divine to a somewhat unanalyzed supporting role" in his examination of the career of George Starkey (924). Cf. William Newman, *Gehennical Fire: The Lives of George Starkey, an American Alchemist in the Scientific Revolution* (Chicago and London: University of Chicago Press, 2002). Another prominent scholar who shares this author's disapproval of the one-sidedness of Newman and his ilk is Michela Pereira of the University of Siena, who in her review of Newman's *Promethean Ambitions: Alchemy and the Quest to Perfect Nature* (Chicago and London: University of Chicago Press, 2004), which appeared in *Renaissance Quarterly* 58.2 (Summer 2005): 678-680, cannot believe the blindness to the hermetic roots of alchemy exhibited by Newman and also by alchemy scholar Pierre Hadot: "Neither author seems to remember that the alchemists themselves used to place…Hermes Trismegistos…at the origin of their art" (680). Cf. P. Hadot, *Le voile d'Isis. Essai sur l'histoire de l'idée de Nature* (Paris: Gallimard, 2004).

Principe and Newman are not alone in their reductionism, nor is Pereira alone in her rejection of it. Consider, for instance, Ole Peter Grell's double review of Pamela Smith's *The Business of Alchemy: Science and Culture in the Holy Roman Empire* (Princeton: Princeton University Press, 1994) and Raphael Patai's *The Jewish Alchemists: A History and Sourcebook* (Princeton: Princeton University Press, 1994), which appeared in *The British Journal for the History of Science* 29.1 (March 1996): 93-94. Grell registers his surprise that Pamela Smith has reduced alchemist J.J. Becher, whose mystical preoccupations led him to hatch Neoplatonic utopian schemes, to an artisan who shed his Paracelsism Principe-style

ever, we wish to go beyond merely pointing out the obvious shortcomings of these otherwise gifted intellectuals' work on the history and pre-history of chemistry.

Principe and Newman, doubtless frustrated with lackluster, ungrounded studies of alchemy (writings inspired by Jung's bizarre theories as well as by earlier 19th century precursors) which see the Great Work as a spiritual quest having no truck with the laboratory, nonetheless fail to find the kind of interpretive balance achieved by scholars such as Joseph P. Farrell, Chiara Crisiani and Bruce T. Moran.[39] For the latter grouping of scholars, alchemy is a spiritual quest that does not exclude the laboratory operations—the physical chemistry; alchemy is seen as a kind of liturgical performance that is at once spiritual *and* scientific. Moreover, it is assumed by this more broadminded group of scholars that various socio-religious contexts are intertwined within both the language used by the alchemists themselves as well as within the alchemists' explicitly stated theories. No such balance is found in Principe and Newman, who dismiss the alchemico-hermetic imagery as mere "expressions of period piety, imprecations to God, [or] exhortations to morality."[40] Strangely enough, in one of their essays Principe and Newman actually go on to admit that their physicalist interpretation is inadequate, though they backtrack abruptly at the last minute, laying responsibility for their immoderate claims at the feet of the equally radical New Agers and their spiritualist forebears: "This is not to say that there was nothing whatsoever akin to a 'spiritual alchemy' in the broad historical spectrum of alchemy. The relationship between alchemy and

---

somewhere around 1650 or so. R.J.W. Evans, in his lukewarm review of Smith's book (*English Historical Review* 111.444 [Nov. 1996]: 1286-1287), also expresses his doubts that Becher "abandoned the system of occult beliefs held by his patrons" to become a proto-capitalist (1287).

39. For Joseph P. Farrell and Chiara Crisiani see the items listed in the bibliography; for Bruce T. Moran see *Distilling Knowledge: Alchemy, Chemistry, and the Scientific Revolution* (Cambridge, MA and London: Harvard University Press, 2005).

40. Lawrence M. Principe and William R. Newman, "Some Problems with the Historiography of Alchemy," in *Secrets of Nature: Astrology and Alchemy in Early Modern Europe*, ed. William R. Newman and Anthony Grafton (Cambridge, MA: MIT Press, 2001), 387-431, at 397.

religion, theology, and spirituality is complex, but still does not countenance the esoteric spiritual school of interpretation."[41]

Besides its historical inaccuracy, Principe and Newman's attempt to de-spiritualize the thousands of documents that comprise the literature of alchemy comes frightfully close to dismissing the entire religio-cultural edifice of Western esotericism simply because it does not concern itself solely with the material world. Not too long ago, this kind of reductionism in science led Michael Polanyi to decry it as a new form of "bigotry" akin to that of religious fundamentalism.[42] It could be argued that Farrell's interpretation of the history of alchemy does what many previous commentators, trapped in either radical spiritualism or radical scientism, have consistently failed to do, for Farrell provides a logically consistent explanation of alchemy which accounts for its continued existence (and possible success[43], in some cases) without turning its practitioners into proto-psychologists or into disinterested chemists in white coats who care nothing for the frock of spirituality or the scepter of power.[44]

Examples in the primary literature that are difficult to fit into either the Jungian "strictly spiritual" approach or the Principean "strictly metallurgical" approach abound, each giving credence to Farrell's (and other recent scholars') more sensible approach. I cannot resist a short list of facts that serve to refute Principe and Newmans' sanitized view of alchemy:

1. The earliest alchemy in China grew organically and directly out of Daoist sects whose attempts to produce

41. Ibid., 397-398.
42. See Michael Polanyi, *Knowing and Being* (Chicago: University of Chicago Press, 1969), 42.
43. See note 38, pg. 64.
44. It is, in fact, quite surprising, considering the "hermeneutics of suspicion"-style revisionism which has held sway in the academic world especially since the twentieth century, that no one has, with a steady hand, followed the alchemical thread back to its power-motivation and its association with particular privileged groups. Doubtless we are seeing a conscious or unconscious perpetuation of the pro-Frankish view of European history, a historiographical orientation called into question in Romanides, *Romeosyne*.

an immortality-granting elixir were thoroughly integrated into their ritual practice.

2. Zosimos of Panopolis, the earliest Egyptian alchemist whose works have survived in a large enough quantity to permit thorough analysis, *recommended meditative religious ascesis, which he stated was the real alchemy*, as a preparation for the concomitant lab work that comprises the Great Work.

3. Roger Bacon, in 13th century England, saw alchemy as a means to determine the characters of individuals and also whole races of people. This would be accomplished, according to Bacon, through alchemical medicines that alter the moral make-up of human beings by overcoming astrally-determined "complexions" that cast a baleful glow over certain races that inhabit certain regions of the globe. The end result, Bacon thought, was an alchemically engineered conversion of the races to the Roman Church!45 Thus, Bacon's Catholicism and his alchemy constitute a seamless whole, alchemy being the scientific answer to the religious problem of the conversion of the races to the Roman Church.

4. A European alchemist from the generation after Bacon, John of Rupescissa (d. 1366), considered alchemical processes to be directly related to his apocalyptic theory of history. For John, alchemical elixirs could extend human life because they were literally "human heaven." William Newman's work on Bacon tries to frame John of Rupescissa's alchemy as an oddball occurrence which preceded a supposed "religious turn" during the generation or so following Bacon.46 Yet many of the earliest

---

45. Zachary Alexander Matus, *Heaven in a Bottle: Franciscan Apolcalypticism and the Elixir, 1250-1360*, PhD diss., Cambridge, MA: Harvard University, 2010, 112.
46. Leah DeVun, *Prophecy, Alchemy, and the End of Time: John of Rupescissa in the Late Middle Ages* (New York: Columbia University Press, 2009), 105: "...[O]ne need not draw a sharp contrast between materialism and spirituality in alchemy. Rupescissa's alchemy was above all material and operative, but it was nevertheless aimed at the solution of spiritual problems: Antichrist, the apocalypse, and the collective salvation of the Christian community. Moreover, Rupescissa built the theory of his alchemy upon spiritual concepts." Here and elsewhere in chapter

European alchemical texts—I am thinking of Michael Scot and his *Ars Alchemie*—mention Hermes by name and speak of transmutation in mystical terms, this fact of course casting serious doubt on Newman's generalization.

One scholar in particular affords a convincing interpretive structure wherein the source material can be assessed. His positions on history and art, while remaining bold and insightful, nevertheless manage to avoid the unsightly extremes of New *Age* and New*man*. His name is Syed Mahdihassan, and to his work we now turn our attention.

Mahdihassan and the Hidden Soul of Alchemy

An Introduction to Mahdihassan's Cosmo-Theanthropic Formulation: The Sliding Scale of Soul

Syed Mahdihassan, in his explorations of perennial symbols and in his re-telling of the origins of alchemy in herbalism, contends that man's historical fixation on gold is best explained in terms of his early animistic worldview.[47] The operative category in this animism is "soul," a concept that despite (or perhaps because of) its vagueness serves as a principle of continuity for early man. This continuity gives man the comforting knowledge that power over the spatial and temporal dimensions is accessible to him. For the faint of heart, it may confer a deep feeling of communion by connecting the individual's personal soul with that of other persons. Ancient man extends this sense of being enmeshed in a web of souls to the cosmic and the divine spheres by ancient man, where differing gradations of soul are manifested. *Soul* is life, but since:

---

six (p. 102-128), DeVun gives ample evidence that, at least in the case of John of Rupescissa, the alchemical code words he used (like "Venus" for iron, etc.) had a religious significance, a fact that William Newman seems to deny.

47. The following summary, where not referenced, draws upon the articles listed in the bibliography under Mahdihassan, Syed.

1. inanimate objects (especially metals) exhibit varied attributes, some conforming more to man's concept of immutability, and others to a kind of chameleon-like mutability; and since:

2. objects such as rocks, plants, and metals can be transformed by applying heat, sometimes producing extracts which produced medicinal and/or stimulating effects if ingested, it seems that:

3. there is *a sliding scale of soul* in the world of nature which cannot be separated from man's internal life, his aspirations for spiritual transcendence. The desire for transcendence is as "natural" as man's fear of death, and indeed, one implies the other. What's more:

4. this sliding scale of cosmic soul is central to man's spiritual (transcendental) aspiration because it is connected to a kind of scientific process (which will be outlined and analyzed below).[48] If Mahdihassan is correct then early man's animism is not the result solely of irrational fears, nor is it pure fantasy. Rather, animism is a creative interpretation of a series of facts that are central to early man's mode of existence.[49] To restate:

    a.   Though early man is conscious that he and his world are mutable, he nevertheless retains an inner sense that he should be immutable, or else he would not have such an aversion to death and mutability.

48. "Thus one and the same agent could confer immortality on man as also make gold. Here ended Animism with the exploitation of soul as such or of an already stored quantum of it. Here also ended Herbalism or the exploitation of herbs as the vehicle of cosmic soul. This was because herbs yielding Kimiya or Soma were scarce or not found at all. The alchemist now proposed to generate the cosmic soul. Animism merely extends the constitution of man to substances thereby endowing each of them with a soul" (Mahdihassan, "Dualistic Symbolism," 57-58).

49. Mercea Eliade, in "The Forge and the Crucible: A Postscript," *History of Religions* 8.1 (1968): 74-88, agrees with Mahdihassan that the first alchemists "were 'experimenters,' not abstract thinkers or erudite scholastics. Their inclination to 'experiment,' however, was not limited to the natural realm. ...[T]he experiments with mineral or vegetal substances pursued a more ambitious goal: to change the alchemist's own mode of being" (77).

b.   Interestingly, the rocks, plants and metals seem to possess inner attributes that correspond to man's concept of immutability/immortality.

c.   Therefore, inner life or "soul" is—for ancient man—a universal reality that is the essence of both nature and man.

d.   Moreover, owing to man's inner constitution, activities which either are a natural expression of his creativity or are essential to his survival (building fires and applying them to substances, grinding up hard substances into powder, etc.), involve refining the raw materials of nature into something...well, *finer*. So far, our chain of thoughts (a.-d.) points to a specific anthropological formula: Man is *he who refines the natural world into greater and greater soulfulness.*

e.   What's more, man's dynamic "soul" relationship with the natural world reveals not only that there are levels of soul, but that *this sliding scale of soul is the defining (even the only) category of existence.* In other words, the category of "person" (which answers the question "who is it?") is subordinated to the category of "soul," the latter category answering the question "how much immutability does it contain?"[50]

f.   Primitive man's concept of "soul" becomes clearer as we analyze it according to traditional categorical distinctions. Interestingly, it seems to straddle all such categories: Soul turns out to be a thing (essence), a process (energy), and a person ("the All"[51]).

---

50. Farrell, *God, History and Dialectic*, 28.
51. "the All": A.J. Hopkins' translation (in *Alchemy, Child of Greek Philosophy* [Morningside Heights, NY: Columbia University Press, 1934], 57) of the inscription accompanying the Ouroboros illustration reproduced in M. Berthelot, *Les origines de l'alchimie* (Paris: Georges Steinheil, 1885), 64.

g.   Since soul can be conceived as the inner
essence or energy of a person or inanimate object,
but without "person" being identified with soul,
we arrive quite naturally at a definition of soul as
the energy that drives the natural processes of a
hypostatic or anhypostatic "container." In short,
through a simple process one can add soul to personal or impersonal natures. Thus, *there are levels
of personhood/soulhood.*

Early man's animistic mentality, as formulated by Mahdihassan, is the foundation of what could be called "cosmic analogy thinking," which we may sum up as follows: The defining
feature of the cosmic analogy is its notion of correspondent
development or movement: There is a dynamic glue which
holds world, man, and God together through its common
motion. A real correspondence or analogy exists between the
strata in that all three levels unfold according to the same pattern, along the same shape or frequency. Just so no mistake is
made about it, let us baldly state that *according to the cosmic
analogy trinity there is not a single thing in the world or above
it that stands outside of the grand mystico-temporal process that
yokes God, man, and cosmos together in the common quest for
cosmo-theanthropic self-realization.*

Mahdihassan's interpretation of alchemy as beginning with
early man's quest to refine the higher "soul of gold"[52] frames the
question in terms of "soul" as equivalent to "essence" or "origin
of soul": "To explain gold in terms of its soul, or of its origin,
is the same as to establish the source of eternal existence or of
creative energy to which immortality is actually due."[53] In this
sense, the method of early alchemy is identical to the method
of Scholastic theology, which, *mutatis mutandis*, identifies the
source of the Persons of the Trinity as Their common energy.
Of course, the supposedly great insight of this Scholastic Trinity is that 1) the Holy Spirit is the energetic bond of love between the Persons, and that 2) this Holy Spirit/bond of love,

---

52. Mahdihassan, "Significance of Ouroboros," 28.
53. Ibid.

viewed from a higher level of analysis, is the divine essence or source of God's existence.[54]

The colossal confusions which the "cosmic analogy" introduces are best illustrated by Mahdihassan's description of what the alchemist must have believed was his deep spiritual task: "If copper is warmed, to drive away its individual soul, and a plant juice, like Soma, dropped on it, the Cosmic Soul in the juice at once diffuses into the metal and makes it everlasting."[55] Notice that the most powerful concept, the notion that sets the alchemical mind apart from other frameworks is the idea of "levels of Soul," or a "sliding scale of soul." Soul can belong to persons, but since the Cosmic Person (God, "the All") includes all other beings, then the only way to maintain a meaningful distinction between divine and non-divine persons is to look at things from another angle, that is, from another *category*.

Just as the Scholastic theologian's eureka moment, his satisfying aesthetic solution to the problem of divine personal existence, was achieved through the individual theologian's own raised consciousness (his realization that the solution to the riddle of the Spirit Who is Person or of the Ghost Who is Holy is that the Person was the divine energy, and that the divine energy was the essence), so the early alchemist realized that to solve the problem of divine Personal (hypostatic) existence is to define the divine Person (God) as the "source of eternal existence or of Creative Energy."[56]

<hr>

54. Note the following passage from Mahdihassan's *Indian Alchemy or Rasayana in the Light of Asceticism and Geriatrics* (New Delhi: Vikas, 1979): "Indian philosophy [and] theoretical alchemy…are founded on Dualism merging into Monism" (ix). Here Madhihassan's insight that a "1" is hiding behind the dyadic "2" is paralleled by Farrell and others' discovery that Western triadology's distinctive note is its "bond of love," which is a movement from 1) initial monism (the radically simple "Deus" or essence), to 2) dualism (Father/Son versus Holy Spirit), and back to monism (the Holy Spirit as the dualistic bond turns out to be the radically simple essence of step one).

55. Mahdihassan, "Significance of Ouroboros," 28.

56. Ibid. Joseph P. Farrell, in chapter nine of his *Giza Death Star Destroyed* (pp. 196-221), offers an analysis of the "eureka moment" of esotericism and Augustinism as it appears in modern (and ancient) physics. See also the appendix to chapter nine (pp. 222-245) for an exposition, in mathematical terms, of esoteric

The Roots of Alchemy and Mysticism According to Mahdihassan: Animism, Dualism and Asceticism.

Mahdihassan's critique of the standard historiography of alchemy can be divided into several distinct strands. First, Mahdihassan, who assumes that alchemical transmutation has never been successful, asserts the following: "If we now accept alchemy to have been the art of synthesizing gold from alloys of base metals, this being impossible, there could never have been any alchemy. Then its history can only be the history of mere claims of synthesizing gold which would be nonsense."[57] This argument gains weight if we add to it Mahdihassan's unique conclusion about the origin of alchemical terminology. For Mahdihassan, the position of Hopkins and others that the term "alchemy" means "art of Egypt" is highly unlikely, for "such a designation would be far too vague for a specialized art like alchemy."[58] The key lies in the Greek term for alchemy and its origin: The Greek term *chemeia* means both "elixir of gold," *and* "art of making gold."[59] Thus, the Greek language did have a word for the elixir or philosopher's stone, but since the historiography assumes a cleavage or even opposition between making gold and a supposedly separate mystical cult of immortality, it has been posited that *chemiea* was mere Egyptian metal making. In fact, if we backtrack to early Chinese sources, we find a well-developed cult of longevity and immortality whose devotees saw in the creating of colloidal cinnabar-gold the apex of their art.

The Chinese cared much more about creating this synthetic red gold, which is a combination of plant and mineral components that were (and still are) believed to have a soul content so rich that it can grant its user immutability and unlimited power over the cosmos.[60] This is the second node of Mahdihas-

cosmo-theanthropology.

57. "Outline of the Beginnings of Alchemy and It's Antecedents," *American Journal of Chinese Medicine* 12 (1984): 32-42, at 32.

58. Ibid., 33.

59. Mahdihassan, "Dualistic Symbolism," 71.

60. "There is gold to strengthen the body and growth-soul of a perennial plant to

The Alchemical Anthropos, from a Medieval Manuscript

make human life correspondingly perennial, whence red-gold became the dual purpose drug of longevity. (-) …[W]hile later on alchemy always tried to make gold and never succeeded, it can be properly redefined as the art that successfully make red-gold or red colloidal gold" (Mahdihassan, "Cinnabar-gold," 97).

san's critique of the standard approach to alchemy: It is untenable to follow the mainstream literature in its assumption that alchemy—a specialized science with a specific mystical symbolism—suddenly popped up in Alexandria with no historical precursors to herald its appearance and to explain from whence came its mythology.[61] Mahdihassan offers an alternative scenario, which, greatly simplified, goes something like this:

1. At the dawn of civilization, when men by and large fed themselves by hunting, elderly warriors who could not keep up with the chase endangered the survival of the entire society.

2 The most humane practice that was developed in response to this disquieting phenomenon was to permanently exile the elderly men into the forest (though in non-wooded areas, ritual execution of the unserviceable hunters seems to have been prevalent).[62] These exiles had to support themselves without hunting, and so began to eat any root or berry that did not kill them.[63]

3 They soon discovered psychotropic drugs that inspired them to compose poems such those in the *Rig Veda*, which may be the oldest writing in existence.[64]

---

61. In the Introduction, we do not follow Mahdihassan's position on the non-Alexandrian origin of alchemy, since documentation in the form of accurately dated texts is lacking. However, we do not rule out Mahdihassan's contention, especially since—to judge by some extant sources—China may have had an extremely ancient tradition of alchemy.

62. Amazingly, Mahdihassan notes that this "inclemency" of early man to the elderly was often extended to women and children. Moreover, the practice of forced exile in hunter-gatherer society appears to have been universal, even extending to German forests where fathers unfit to hunt were beheaded by sons in ceremonies that, as a consolation prize, promised the aged and infirm a ticket to Valhalla (*Indian Alchemy*, 6-8).

63. Of course, there was only one way to find out which plants were lethal, and that was the old-fashioned taste test. Doubtless, individuals learned from others' mistakes, thereby creating a body of knowledge about plants and their properties.

64. S. Mahdihassan, "Alchemy, Chinese Versus Greek, An Etymological Approach: A Rejoinder," *American Journal of Chinese Medicine* 16.1-2 (1988): 83-86, at 85.

4. Mahdihassan identifies Soma with the amphetamine *Ephedra sinica*, and believes that Soma and other like substances were at the heart of the longevity cults ubiquitous in the ancient world.

These cults started with "simples," like Soma, which were revered as drugs of rejuvenation and even of immortality. The Chinese believed that these simples, when combined in specific ways with plants and metals, resulted in a synthetic superdrug of longevity which was "the first synthetic drug known to history and it was red colloidal gold."[65]

5 From China to India, from India to the Arab world, from the Arabs (and later the Indians themselves) to Copts and Hellenized Greeks in Alexandria, and thence to Western Europe— his is Mahdihassan's proposed scheme of cultural transmission of the alchemical cult of longevity.[66]

This idea of an unbroken line of alchemical succession— from China, through Indian and Arab mediators, ending up in early medieval Europe by way of Alexandria—is the third and final strand of Mahdihassan's theory of alchemy that we

On Soma cf. Wendy Doniger O'Flaherty, ed. and trans., *The Rig Veda: An Anthology* (London: Penguin, 1981), 121ff. Esp. note the solar, doxa association of Soma, which one passage describes "as shining or golden and dwelling in the sky" (177). As for the power connection, which will be examined fully below, see ibid., p. 129: "Ecstatic with Soma I shattered the nine and ninety fortresses of Śambara all at once, finishing off the inhabitant as the hundredth...". Also see connections between Soma and the materia prima doctrine of alchemy as argued in Terence McKenna, *Food of the Gods: The Search for the Original Tree of Knowledge, A Radical History of Plants, Drugs, and Human Evolution* (New York: Bantam, 1992), 97ff.

As for Mahdihassan, he has no doubt that Soma is the ephedra plant, known as "Haoma among the Zoroastrains [sic]. A juice is given as few drops to a child newly born. This custom exist even to-day and the plant used is ephedra. Thus ephedra as Haoma has an uninterrupted history of the use of ephedra as Haoma" (Mahdihassan, "The Seven Theories Identifying the Soma Plant," *Ancient Science of Life* 9.2 (October 1989): 86-89, at 86. Madihassan cites Jivanji Jamshedji Modi, *The Religious Ceremonies and Customs of the Parsees* (Mazagon, Bombay: British India Press, 1922), 303.

65. Mahdihassan, "Outline," 40.

66. Mahdihassan, "Alchemy and Its Fundamental Terms in Greek, Arabic, Sanskrit, and Chinese," *Indian Journal of History of Science* 16.1 (May 1981): 64-76, at 70-71.

will consider. The unbroken succession theory is significant because it offers the only viable explanation in the literature for the continued existence of a "power" element, associated equally with longevity/immortality and ascetico-mysticism, from ancient China until the present day.

Mahdihassan and others supply us with ample evidence that alchemy, in each of its cultural phases, was never mere gold-making. In China, it was the Golden-Man, he who held the secret of the Great Work, "who could say 'my life is within my own control and not heaven's,' as pronounced by Ko-Hung, the Chinese alchemist...".[67] Also finding its beginning in China was "potable gold," which is still used there by some as a drug of rejuvenation.[68] Apropos the Arab cultural phase, Mahdihassan notes that the surname "al-Sufi" originated with Jabir ibn Hayyan, "Sufi" referring to an ascetic Way parallel to the Chinese Dao. To suggest that Jabir's life's work was some materialistic lust for gold is thus quite untenable, especially since he often speaks of the elixir as a medicine *par excellence*.[69] As for Greek alchemy, the earliest record of the art as practiced in Alexandria,

---

67. Mahdihassan, "Alchemy, Chinese Versus Greek," 86. Interior citation F.S. Taylor, *The Alchemists* (New York: Henry Schuman, 1949), 38.

68. On Chinese potable gold, see Joseph Needham, *Science and Civilisation in China, Volume 5. Chemistry and Chemical Technology, Part 2. Spagyrical Discovery and Invention: Magisteries of Gold and Immortality* (Cambridge: Cambridge University Press, 1974), 68ff.

69. Mahdihassan, "Alchemy, in Its Proper Setting, with Jinn, Sufi, and Suffa, as Loan Words form the Chinese." *Iqbal* 7.3 (1959): 1-10, at 3. Cf. idem, "Jabir's Magic Sqare as the Symbol of Venus Which Was the Eight Cornered Star," *Hamdard Medicus* 34.3 (July-September 1991): 46-48. Note also that the notion of the elixir as an agent giving one the wherewithal to "fly about," in effect transcending the limits of space, which we noticed in the Rig Veda (O'Flaherty, 137: "I am huge, huge! flying to the cloud."), later becomes the Taoist "Kimia [which] made its user not only immortal but also capable of flying about; man became a jinn, which again is a Chinese word otherwise pronounced as Hsien" (Mahdihassan, "Alchemy, in Its Proper Setting," 2). Here we see the journey of the Vedic Soma to the Chinese "pill of immortality" and finally to the D'jini of the *Arabian Nights*. Though he is wrong in his notion that the Alexandrians cared nothing for the mystical elements of alchemy, scholar Tenney L. Davis says the Chinese "were attempting to make real gold artificially, not because of its intrinsic value but because of its magical efficacy. They wished to compound from it edible pills of immortality by the eating of which they would be converted into Hsien or benevolent immortals" (Davis, "Origins of Alchemy," 557).

the *Dialogue of Cleopatra*, "speaks of Medicine-of-Life, and of resurrecting the dead. Taylor continues to quote the text stating that the alchemists were asked by Cleopatra 'to look at the nature of plants whence they come [and at the] divine Water (which) gives them a body in a being. (—) Here is clearly a Medicine-of-Life and its function is to resurrect the dead".[70] If more evidence is needed that Greek alchemy was equal parts gold-making and mysticism, insists Mahdihassan, we need only turn to the *Corpus Hermetica*—which drips spiritualism on every page—and to the Alexandrian Zossimus of Panopolis (fl. 300 A.D.), whose Gnostic brand of metallurgy "established an enduring connection between practical laboratory work and spiritual perfection."[71]

Moving now to the last phase—the transmission of Arab and Greek alchemy to Europe—we find ample evidence that the mystical theory of alchemy continued and thrived. In fact, if we follow Principe and Newman's notion that iatrochemical alchemy appeared only with Paracelsus (1493-1541), we can make no historical sense of the thirteenth century debate in Europe over the legitimacy of alchemy. The controversy hinged upon whether or not the alchemist could *match or exceed God's creative power*. Writers involved in the fracas such as Roger Bacon (c. 1220-1292) spent their lives repeating over and over that alchemical gold was the medicine of medicines, the cure-all drug. As we touched on earlier, Bacon carried on the tradition of potable gold that flourished in the later Middle Ages and that persists, according to some sources, even to this very day.[72] So, Bacon's thirteenth century iatrochemistry disproves Principie and Newman's wild assertion that *iatroche-*

---

70. Mahdihassan, "Outline," 33.

71. Tara E. Nummedal, "Alchemy. Europe and the Middle East," *New Dictionary of the History of Ideas in New Dictionary of the History of Ideas*, ed. Maryanne Cline Horowitz, 6 vols. (Detroit: Thompson Gale, 2005), 1.40-44, at 41.

72. Nummedal, "Alchemy," 42. On the manufacture and consumption of potable gold at as late a date as the seventeenth century, note the following passage from Mendelsohn, "Alchemy and Politics": Otto Faber was "summoned to England by Charles in 1660/1, [and] he eventually joined the Society of Friends, through whose networks he distributed his cordials, and was imprisoned as a dangerous 'maker of Quakers' and deported in 1667. A few years later he was back in England, physician to aristocrats, called in with his *aurum potabile* to the bedside of the archbishop during his last illness" (76).

meia appeared in Europe over three hundred years later. Not only that, but—to repeat—the crux of the thirteenth century controversy over alchemy was its inherent teaching that the alchemist gains a power that equals or exceeds that of God Himself. Whether historians of science like it or not, many of the alchemical texts translated from Arabic into Latin discussed these mystical themes at great length, the power-motive never straying far from the surface.[73]

---

73. Let it be noted that our argument against the "lust for gold" interpretation does not entail a denial that some individuals—with a power motivation—wanted to make mass quantities of gold. Ogrinc cites at least one King of England whose alchemical interests pointed in this area. This royal example is paralleled by that of the "puffers," who were hack alchemists who did not seem to be in touch with the deeper significance of the Great Work. However, none of this can stand as evidence against our thesis or for the "goldlust" thesis, for 1) the fact that "puffers" were derided as uncomprehending misers proves that many believed in alchemy's mystical side, and 2) the source material does not provide anything like an objective view of these "puffers." Were they really so obtuse? The authors of these anti-puffer sources were also known for their jealousy of and hostility toward other alchemists with whom they were in competition for patronage and prestige.

Chapter Four

Icons of the *Magnum Opus*

Harmony is the key of the World.

-C onfucius[74]

...[H]umans have been able to discover the divine nature and how to make it.

-H ermes Trimegistus[75]

Keeping the insights of Farrell and Mahdihassan in mind, let us dive into the elusive but powerful world of alchemical imagery or iconography. First, we turn our attention to the 6th century B.C., when a seldom remembered upheaval occurred—we will term it "the Ionian revolution"— which rocked the Mediterranean world, the Asian continent, and possibly other parts of Europe as well.[76] H.E. Stapleton affords a glimpse into the agitated scene:

> It was a century marked by a sudden outburst of revolu-
> tionary thought along the great highway of the Steppes
> over which—for, probably, thousands of years—the tide
> of humanity has ebbed and flowed. (-) In China, the lead-

---

74. Cited in H.E. Stapleton and G.J.W., "Ancient and Modern Aspects of Pythago-reanism," *Osiris* 13 (1958), 12-53, at 34.

75. Copenhaver, Hermetica, 90.

76. We have taken the phrase "Ionian revolution" from A.R. Utke, who uses the term in a very narrow sense. For Utke, the Ionian upheaval is the scientific, ra-tional turn signaled by the Pre-Socratics. In this essay the revolution is consid-ered in its broader aspect, as a worldwide spiritual and cultural shift. For Utke's definition see his "Alchemy and the Concept of Ultimate Reality and Meaning," Ultimate Reality and Meaning 27.1 (2004): 51-69, at 54; and also his "The Cosmic Holism Concept: An Interdisciplinary Tool In the Quest For Ultimate Reality and Meaning," *Interdisciplinary Studies In the Understanding of Ultimate Reality and Meaning* 17.3 (1986): 134-155.

er and guider of man's thought was Confucius: in India, Gautama, the Buddha: in Iran, Zoroaster: in Greece, Pythagoras: and, however different the gospel was that each of these men preached, their teaching may be summed up in the Pauline phrase that henceforward men should "walk not after the flesh but after the Spirit."[77]

Stapleton goes on to pinpoint exactly what the connection between all of these thinkers was: A matter/spirit dualism which viewed ultimate truth as correct belief (ortho-doxy) about the "third thing"—the latter being *the formula that gives one knowledge of the true plane of interaction between the spiritual and material realms, the knower of which is able to ascend to the uncreated realm, thereby attaining all of its attributes or powers.*[78] Pythagoras is known to have been a primary inspirer of Plato, and through the great Athenian sage, Pythagoras became also a forefather to the hermetists, to the Neoplatonists, and especially to the Renaissance poets and theologians who traced their philosophical family tree back to him.

A kind of mystical geometry was Pythagoras' "third thing," his divine/earthly tangent, and it began with a conception of God as an utterly transcendent, radically simple unity, or *Monas*. For Pythagoras and his followers, the *Monas*, or "Divine Unity" could not be represented or circumscribed in any way. Despite this staunch belief in the *Monas'* utter transcendence—and this is one of the most earth-shaking, influential ideas ever conceived—Pythagoras allowed that the *Monas* could be indicated, however provisionally, by the simplest marking conceivable—a point.[79] Though it was believed that the *Monas* was a

77. Stapleton, "Aspects," 26.

78. Ibid., 26-27. Stapleton sees Pythagoreanism as a unique and powerful version of what we have, following Farrell, called the "dialectic of oppositions." J.E. Raven's admirable *Pythagoreans and Eleatics: An Account of the Interaction Between the Two Opposed Schools during the Fifth and Early Fourth Centuries B.C.* (Amsterdam: Adolf M. Hakkert, 1966) is cited by Stapleton (26) for its searching examination of Pythagoreanism's "Eternal Dualism" (Raven, *Pyth. and Eleatics,* 18).

79. It must be admitted that we have no good reason to think that Pythagoras had any qualms about representing the Monas in a geometrical form. In fact, ascertaining exactly what Pythagoras believed is an interpretive pickle without rival (see the "Introduction" for more details). It is quite possible that he saw no

dimensionless, uncontainable, transcendent Unity which could not be positioned, the attempt to represent this notion of God as a dot on a page (or other surface) undercut this purpose in an exceedingly subtle manner.[80] Here are just a few of the (perhaps unintended) implications of the *Monas* as inscribed dot:

1. The non-positioned One has now been positioned, and can be circumscribed or otherwise limited through its relation to other inscribed points or figures.

2. Though it is not perfectly circular, a small blot on a page (or a small pebble in the sand) appears to be a tiny circle to the naked eye, as Robert Hooke noted (see fig. 3, page 159),[81] and we all know that a circle, however small, is divisible (and expandable).

3. As any geometer knows, a circle is created first by fastening a compass arm upon a point, and then by tracing a flowing point with the other compass arm, the resultant line being at all places equidistant from the initial point. Thus, the circle is by definition composite, being comprised of a center and a periphery. To translate this into cosmo-theological terms, God has a center and a periphery, and is thus composed of parts. S.K. Heninger speaks eloquently about these theological and philosophical consequences of the Pythagorean *Monas*:

contradiction between the One's utter transcendence and its immanent reflection in creation. For example, if we flash forward several centuries Blessed Augustine, in De Trinitate, does not seem to be bothered by the idea of a real analogy of the essence of the Holy Trinity in nature. In fact, he is rather well pleased with his "trinity-spotting" project, though it is not clear if Augustine is elevating his trinitarian speculations to the realm of dogma. Relevant passages from *De Trinitate* have been collected and analyzed by Fr. John S. Romanides in his "Yahweh of Glory According to the 1st, 2nd, and 9th Ecumenical Councils," Theologia 71 (2000): 133-199.

80. Mahdihassan makes the astute connection between the Pythagorean "point-circle" and the Brahman-Atman dichotomy in the Upanishads: "...[A]ll forms preceded from the formless. (-) ...Brahman at the beginning was non-existent... but full of existence" ("A Positive Conception of the Divinity Emanating From a Study of Alchemy," *Iqbal Review* 10 [1969]: 77-125, at 95).

81. Robert Hooke, *Micrographia, or Some Physiological Descriptions of Minute Bodies Made by Magnifying Glasses with Observations and Inquiries Thereupon* (London: Martyn and Allestry, 1665), 1-3.

The first step is recognition of a paradox: although unlimited and eternal, the monad, being a unit, is represented in the terms of Pythagorean number by a point, which of course has no dimension—indeed, has no existence except as a concept. (-) But when a number is imposed upon space and fixed in position, it acquires extension; when number is impressed upon matter, it acquires physicality. Therefore, since the point as concept is correlative with the number 1, it assumes substance when it becomes 1 something—for example, 1 dot in a diagram, or 1 stone, or 1 tree, or 1 man. In this fashion, the monad, infinite and eternal though it may be, is placed in relationship to each item in nature.[82]

Now that God has exhaled, expanding Himself into a circle which surrounds Him, He wishes now to move his center, his point, to the periphery, thereby creating another circle, a second exhalation to mirror the first. The resultant picture (fig. 4, page 159) of two identical interlocking circles with a horizontal, mandorla shaped tangent-vector between them, represents the Pythagorean trinity. The *Monas*-point contains this trinitarian development within It, for 1) the circle presupposes a point, 2) the circle is itself a flowing point, and thus 3) any part of the periphery can become a new circle, which nonetheless remains connected in a symmetrical unity with the initial point-circle. God's exhalation or expansion into geometric extension is a necessary expression of God's essence; it is the expression of God's energy or activity, for otherwise God would remain sterile and unproductive of qualities and attributes, as Jung intimates: "Three is an unfolding of the One to a condition where it can be known—unity becomes recognizable; had it not been resolved into the polarity of the One and the Other, it would have remained fixed in a condition devoid of every quality. Three therefore appears as a suitable synonym for a process of development in time, and thus forms a parallel to the self-revelation of the Deity as the absolute One unfolded into Three."[83]

---

82. Heninger, *Harmony*, 78-79.
83. Jung, *Psychology*, 119. The notion of a divine barrenness that is overcome

What is interesting here is that the third term, the copula or connecting factor in the Pythagorean trinity, is the concept of unity as a radical simplicity which is present in the point from the beginning as its unconscious *telos*, and which unity under-lies the second, incarnational-cosmological step (the first cir-cle, or the Logos-Son) as its real meaning and potential. This notion of the third term as the radically simple inner meaning or reality of the second (and by extension, the first) term, if we recall Jung's comment above, is also equivalent to the activa-tion of Divine energy or power, which is shown to be the undi-vided, uncreated substance from which sprang all of physical reality. To follow the logic to its unavoidable conclusion: The prime matter, the undifferentiated substrate of Divine power cannot be distinguished from the essence of God, for both are radically simple, uncreated, and, most importantly, possess/express every attribute of the Divine: immortality, omnipo-tence, immutability, etc.

The foregoing is a first step toward substantiating our con-tention that the Platonic/Pythagorean trinity is an expression *par excellence* of alchemico-esoteric traditions which can be traced back to the early dualism of Indo-European and Asi-atic societies; and, further, that this tradition was nurtured in the Middle Ages through the Neoplatonic filioquist triadology of the Christian West. The artisans and their aristocratic pa-trons who remained, century after century, avid practitioners of alchemy did so because their theological and philosophical purview pointed them toward what was, for them, the highest goal of all, the Great Work of transmutation, which gave man power over the cosmos. If we trace alchemy back to its early

---

through subsequent activation or differentiation is contained in the alchemical symbol of the Cosmic egg: "It contains the germ of all that exists, the creation and the creator. In an egg its contents are not developed" ("Alchemy and Its Chinese Origin As Revealed by Its Etymology, Doctrines and Symbols," *Iqbal Review* 7 (1966): 22-58, at 34). Mahdihassan marvels at an illustration ("Positive Conception," 112) depicting the cosmos as two fish swimming in a circular sea surrounding a central point, which the artist expanded so that it looked like the sun's disc. For Madhihassan the ingenuity of the artist was his depiction of the divine point as unknowable (the disc is plain and unadorned) and yet also knowable (it is a disc and is monochromatic, as the sun is often represented).

history in China, we find much evidence that the elixir was seen as a universal soul-force that can become incarnate in an mineral or animal body: "[T]he cosmic soul is a universal life element; (-) it can also put life in a tottering dynasty which can retain power and continue to rule longer. (-) Accordingly 'any manifestation of a change in nature meant that something was about to happen in the human world and (conversely) proper behaviour on the part of Man would also influence the way of Heaven."[84] Our thesis, if nothing else, finally offers a plausible explanation for the otherwise inexplicable lack of conflict between the Latin Christian Church and the alchemists in the Middle Ages. Though she fails to draw any far-reaching conclusions, Ursula Szulakowska notes that "in fifteenth century Canterbury...the monks had access to the largest collection of [alchemical] texts in Europe."[85] Vladimir Karpenko's befuddlement at this Latin Christian-alchemical rapprochement is typical of much mainstream literature: "Surprisingly at the moment [of the] introduction of alchemy these two ideologies did not collide, and did not do [so] even later, in spite of the fact that the claims of alchemy to be able to achieve in the laboratory the same [results that are produced in] nature...was in obvious contradiction to the teaching of the Church. Because, in other words, alchemists pretended [to do] something [that] was an activity reserved exclusively to God himself."[86]

---

84. Mahdihassan, "Dualistic Symbolism," 60. Interior citation Cheng Te-K'un, "Yin-Yang Wu-Hsing and Han Art," *Harvard Journal of Asiatic Studies* 20 (1957): 162-186 at 162.

85. Ursula Szulakowska, "Patronage in Relation to Alchemical Illustration in the Early Italian Renaissance: Three Case Studies," *Artium Academiae Scintiarium Hungaricae* 35 (1990/1992): 169-180, at 178. Szulakowska cites Pearl Kibre, "The Intellectual Interests Reflected in Libraries of the 14C and 15C," *Journal of the History of Ideas* 7.3 (June 1946): 258-297, at 294.

86. Karpenko, "Metals," 106. Cf. Ogrinc, 114-117, on the medieval Papacy's involvement in alchemy. A discussion of human creativity as an analogue of divine creation in the *Corpus Hermeticum* is found in Albanese, *Republic of Mind*, 28-29; for an elucidation of the creator/Creator analogy in Jakob Boehme and Sir Isaac Newton see Van Alan Herd, *The Concept of Ungrund in Jakob Boehme (1575-1624)*, (M.A. thesis, University of Oklahoma, 2003), 67-68. Lest we get the false impression that alchemy was strictly a Roman Catholic affair, Allen G. Debus, in "Changing Perspectives On the Scientific Revolution," *Isis* 89.1 (March 1998), 66-81, at 77, points out that after the Reformation Paracelsism was more com-

Of the many primary sources that show an obvious melding of Western Christianity with alchemio-hermeticism, *The Book of the Holy Trinity* (Das Buch der heiligen Dreifaltigkeit)[87] seems most remarkable, since it included, true to its title, an alchemical triadology and a concomitant Christology.[88]

Though the foregoing picture of alchemy we have put forth does collide with many voices across the academic spectrum, it must also be stated that our thesis about the prehistoric origin of alchemy and its basis in dualistic theology and "prime matter" physics is in concord with a minority position in the mainstream literature, a representative voice being Harry J. Sheppard, who defined alchemy as "the art of liberating parts of the Cosmos from temporal existence and achieving perfection which, for metals is gold, and for man, longevity, then immortality, and, finally, redemption."[89] Our proposed mixture of 1) Christianity, with its notion of a selfless love for the world, and 2) alchemical esotericism, with its ambiguous goal of power as a reward for the worthy, also explains the historiographical confusion over the motivations of alchemists, best expressed by Michela Pereira, who wrote: "Hermes' teachings...led alchemists...to the discovery of the innermost *arcana naturae*, whose possession was eagerly desired at least from late Antiquity onward in *order to improve humanity's (or simply one's own) life*."[90] One wonders whether or not Pereira saw the irony in positing that alchemists were trying to help either 1) everyone else or 2) only themselves, as if these two motivations are tantamount; or whether she subscribes to some eudaemonistic ethic that sees no contradiction between selfishness and selflessness.

---

mon amongst Protestants than Catholics, though the latter certainly remained alchemically inclined. Cf. Martha Baldwin, "Alchemy and the Society of Jesus in the Seventeenth Century: Strange Bedfellows," *Ambix* 40 (1993): 41-64.

87. Uwe Junker, ed., *Das "Buch der Heiligen Dreifaltigkeit"* (Köln: Institut für Geschichte der Medizin der Universität, 1986).

88. For background and commentary on the Buch, see *Ogrinc*, 121-122, 127.

89. H.J. Sheppard, "European Alchemy in the Context of a Universal Definition," in *Die Alchemie in der europaischen Kultur- und wissenschaftsgeschichte* (Wiesbaden: Otto Harrassowitz, 1986), 13-17, at 17.

90. Michela Pereira, "Alchemy and Hermeticism: An Introduction To This Issue," *Early Science and Medicine* 5.2 (2000): 115-120, at 117, emphasis added.

Michael Maier's *Atalanta fugiens* (Oppenheim, 1618) gives us a pictorial demonstration of the alchemical process of producing the *lapis philosophorum* in his famous illustration of a sage "squaring the circle" (fig. 5, page 160). The sage, beginning with the point, produces a small circle. The duality of point and periphery, for Maier's sage, is best expressed by the male-female dichotomy, which we previously discussed in the introduction to this essay and in our section on Mahdihassan. Next the dual circle is expanded into a square, since "from every simple body the four elements must be separated."[91] Fittingly, the third stage of the Great Work reveals the ultimate meaning of the alchemical trinity: "By the transformation of the square into a triangle they teach that one should bring forth spirit, body and soul, which then appear in three brief colours before the redness."[92] This is the big tie-in, man's tripartite composition being related to the three sides of the triangle (which obliquely refers to the Father, Son, and Holy Spirit of the *Scutum fidei*) as well as to the three stages of the universal process, the job of recapitulating or re-engineering creation through prime matter. The universal scope of the alchemist's resultant power is shown in the fourth and final step, the larger circle which touches the two lower corners of the triangle. This trinity-encompassing circle is "an immutable redness," a power over the cosmos, a power that can transmute all things into its own radically simple essence.[93] This doctrine of the alchemical production of prime matter as the "squaring of the circle" is more than a search for shiny metals, as Eric LaVigne stresses: "If the alchemist knew the formula that would square the circle…then he or she would have the key to the creation of the material world from the spiritual world, of the finite from the infinite. *The process could then also be made to go the other way, from the material world to the spiritual world and back again.*"[94]

---

91. Alexander Roob, *The Hermetic Museum: Alchemy and Mysticism* (Köln: Tachen, 1997), 466.
92. Ibid.
93. Ibid.
94. LaVigne, "Squaring," 39, emphasis added.

Another alchemical work, the anonymous *Aurora con-surgens* (early 16th century), links the squaring of the circle witnessed in Maier's illustration to the Carolingian "Shield of Faith" (fig. 6, page 160).[95] Notice that the Divine Persons are color-coded, the white Dove symbolizing the "whitening" process which follows the Son's initial "blackening" process. The "immutable redness" alluded to in Maier's illustration is here associated with the central circle of the Shield, the one which normally is labeled "God," and which symbolizes the simple, uncompounded essence of God. As is known from al-chemical texts, this final step of "reddening" is the goal of the Great Work, and the research of Syed Mahdihassan, as treated above, has shown the age-old connection in the mind of man between intense redness and Soul-energy, the latter associated, naturally, with prime matter and its divine power.[96]

---

95. Roob, *Hermetic Museum*, 473.
96. Madhdihassan, "Cinnabar-Gold," 94.

Conclusion

In this section we have traced the development of different notions of threeness in the history of Western esotericism and—briefly—in the mystical theology of Eastern Orthodoxy. Our examination calls into question the conclusions of much mainstream writing on esotericism through fresh readings of primary sources and new looks at previously neglected secondary writings. Though many important points were developed along the way, our focus remained what we termed the cosmo-theanthropic trinity, which seems to have been universal in the ancient world (excepting some pockets of Judaic culture), and remains, we contend, the basis of Western esotericism, as the history of alchemy evinces. In the West, alchemy became intertwined with Christian theology in the centuries following the life of Blessed Augustine of Hippo Regius. So, why should anyone living in today's world care about these matters? The significance of our thesis becomes readily apparent when we consider the continuity of two traditions—alchemy and Augustinian theology—as they have existed from their origins to today. Indeed, up to the writing of this book, the Western world has produced no successor to the *Augustinian esoteric paradigm*, or at least no successor has been found that overturns the fundamental presuppositions of this worldview. The next two chapters will aim at fleshing out this Augustinian esoteric paradigm, though I must beg the reader's patience, the directions we hope to trace being accessible only through the most circuitous of indirect paths.

2

"THE MAN WHO WOULD BE MORE THAN KING": PHILIP THE FAIR'S THEL-LEMMA

thelemaᴳ reek word meaning t' he will." [1]

dilemma—A situation that requires one to choose between two equally balanced alternatives.

---

1. This chapter's subtitle is in no wise an attempt at connecting King Philip the Fair with Crowley's occult philosophy/organization called "Thelema." In fact, I knew nothing about Crowley's Thelema until the latter stages of revising this book. Hopefully my pun on the Greek word for "will" does not create more confusion than amusement.

Philip the Fair (Philippe le Bel) was, as Philip IV, King of France from 1285 until his death in November 1314.

Chapter Five

An Introduction to Philip the Fair's World

"**A** civilization, like a human being, has a will to live, but it may also arrive at the neurotic condition of having a will to die." Medievalist Norman F. Cantor spoke thusly of the late thirteenth century, that most exhilarating of epochs, which erected grand thought systems that seemed to generate at least as much tension as satisfaction.[1] The rediscovery of Aristotle had inspired St. Thomas Aquinas and others to construct a more inclusive, more synthetic religio-philosophical edifice than had previously been thought possible. However, many became increasingly discontent with the new synthesis, most notably the Ockamists, who called into question the convoluted Thomistic scheme, with its proliferation of categories and relations. Has the incorporation of more and more concepts and terms into the earlier, simpler Scholasticism really drawn us any closer to the truth? Such thoughts doubtless plagued the late thirteenth century mind.

More generally, the thirteenth century seemed to have introduced a new *kind* of tension into all areas of life. New practices were developing in art, religion, and politics; these innovations were often reactions against the perceived constrictiveness of the "new traditions." Heresy, though it had never really abated, was then raging ever more strongly in the West. The Inquisition and the Albigensian Crusade head up the thirteenth century's list of dubious accomplishments. From these facts we are tempted to generalize (thought it may seem too obvious to state) that societies undergoing a disconcerting amount of

---

1. Norman F. Cantor, *Medieval History: The Life and Death of a Civilization*, 2nd ed. (New York: Macmillan; London: Collier-Macmillan, 1969), 505.

change often counter by *creating new scapegoats*, an activity which, at its most intense core, turns *mystical*. But, it is true that we would not know of the thirteenth century's staunch inquisition-mindedness had there not been a plethora of antagonistic heretical groups with which the thirteenth century European establishment had to contend.

Perhaps even more obnoxious to established society were those elements that burst on the scene from *within* groups that could not be easily sifted out and ostracized, and which thus may be termed *novel orthodoxies*. These "new traditions," ironically, provoked new heresies, chief amongst them the reemergence of the concept of patriotism in the West. In the wake of Philip IV of France's war against the rebellious Flemish, an anonymous preacher declared that the people should fight for King Philip not because of any mere feudal obligation, but rather because the King was the head of the kingdom, and all of his subjects were members of this body, which was "*patria*," or "the fatherland." Further, this zealous homilist proclaimed that the basis of the Frankish kings' power, and the reason that all should defend it, was "the saintly character…of the *nobiles et sancti reges Francorum*."[2] Ever since the exploits of Charlemagne, the sermon went on, the Frankish nobility had never ceased to produce saints, as evinced by the "royal touch"—the French kings' ability, shared by no other kings or nobles the world over, of curing scrofula by the touch of their hands.[3]

---

2. Ernst H. Kantorowicz, "Pro Patria Mori in Medieval Political Thought," *American Historical Review* 56.3 (April 1951): 472-492, at 483. Kantorowicz cites Dom Jean Leclerq, "Un sermon prononcé pendant la guerre de Flandre sous Philippe le Bel," *Revue du moyen âge latin* 1 (1945): 165-172, as the original source for the sermon.
3. For a full bibliography on the royal touch see Frank Barlow, "The King's Evil," *English Historical Review* 95.374 (Jan. 1980): 3-27. The classic work on the subject remains Marc Bloch, *Les rois thaumaturges: etude sur le caractere surnaturel attribue a la puissance royale, particulirement en France el en Angleterre* (Paris and Stasbourg: Publications de la Faculte des lettres de l'Universite de Strasbourg, fasc. I9, 1924); An English translation by J. E. Anderson was later published as *The Royal Touch: Sacred Monarchy and Scrofula* in England and France (London, 1973). On Philip the Fair's promotion and administration of the royal touch see idem, *Le rois*, 105-110; and Elizabeth A. R. Brown, "The Prince is Father of the King: The Character and Childhood of Philip the Fair of France." *Mediaeval Studies* 49 (1987): 282-334, at 332.

Though many like our zealous homilist claimed that these notions of patriotism and royal healing had been around since time immemorial, not everyone was buying, notably an exasperated Pope and a number of harried non-Frankish peoples on the outlying reaches of the *Regnum Francorum* such as the Flemish, which had just been brought to heel by a haughty King Philip IV early in the fourteenth century.[4]

In fact, Philip the Fair can be seen as exemplar *par excellence* of the inner and outer tensions rife in the thirteenth and fourteenth centuries, tensions that were not unrelated to the apocalyptic hopes that inspired the alchemical dreams of Roger Bacon or John of Rupescissa. However, if we trace the political history of Europe backward in time from Philip the Fair's reign into the origins of the Frankish kingdom, the earthshaking import of Philip's reign for all subsequent history becomes apparent. Specifically, our backward glance shows that Philip's reign was the endpoint of a long development, one facet of which was the centralization of power in the hands of the French crown and the concomitant transformation of the Frankish king into the single most powerful authority in the world.[5] We must not forget that a few centuries before Philip came to power, the king of France was little more than a feudal lord who ruled only the narrow strip of land that was the Ile-de-France, though he was the nominal ruler over much more.

---

4. On new secularizing policies under Philip the Fair including bureaucratic expansion, universal conscription, and state taxation see Joseph R. Strayer, "The Laicization of French and English Society in the Thirteenth Century," Speculum 15.1 (Jan. 1940): 76-86. On Philip's innovative policy of "defense of the realm" see Joseph R. Strayer, "Defense of the Realm and Royal Power in France," in *Studi in orore di Gino Luzzato* (Milan, 1949), 1.289-296; and Gabrielle M. Spiegel, "'Defense of the Realm': Evolution of a Capetian Propaganda Slogan," *Journal of Medieval History* 3 (1977): 115-134.

5. On the reign of Philip the Fair as the apex of Frankish kingly power, see E.A.R. Brown, "Prince is Father": "During Philip's reign was promoted a conception of the French monarchy far grander and more militant than had ever before been advanced: the king of France was presented as 'the leader of the cause of God and the Church and the champion of all Christendom'" (283). Also pertinent is Joseph R. Strayer's "France: the Holy Land, the Chosen People and the Most Christian King," in *Medieval Statecraft and the Perspectives of History: Essays by Joseph R. Strayer*, ed. J. F. Benton and T. H. Bisson (Princeton, NJ: Princeton University Press, 1971), 300-314.

Ironically, the ascendancy of the French crown to almost un-
heard of heights of power was paralleled by the transformation
of the Pope from local Italian figurehead to purported ruler
over all spiritual and worldly authorities.[6]

For scholar Joseph P. Farrell the long historical process
which culminated with the power contest between Pope Boniface VIII and Philip the Fair can be traced to the theological
formulations of Blessed Augustine of Hippo. While it may seem
strange to suggest that the writings of a single man could carry
enough weight to shape all subsequent theological discourse
for an entire civilization, let it be noted that a great number
of authorities, both pro and con, name Augustine as the most
important Church Father for Western Christianity. Protestant theologian Paul Tillich takes for granted that Blessed Augustine "is the foundation of everything the West has to say,"
and the Roman Catholic Augustino Trape proclaims that the
bishop of Hippo Regius is "undoubtedly the greatest of the Fathers…".[7] Of the many innovations propagated by Augustine,
possibly the most significant for the history of *sacerdotium et
regnum* in the West was his identification of the divine essence
of the Holy Trinity with the radically simple "One" of Plotinus.[8] The unity of the Augustino-Platonic essence precedes

---

6. On the origin of the papal claims in the papal reform movement see Aris-
teides Papadakis and John Meyendorff, *The Christian East and the Rise of the Papacy* (Crestwood, NY: St. Vladimir's Seminary Press, 1994), 1-67. The outstanding
scholarship of Walter Ullmann on the history of the papacy is the best place
to start for both a diachronic as well as a synchronic analysis of the institution.
See Walter Ullmann, *The Growth of Papal Government in the Middle Ages: A Study
in the Ideological Relation of Clerical to Lay Power*, 3rd ed. (London: Methuen,
1970 [1955]); and idem, *A Short History of the Papacy in the Middle Ages*, 2nd ed.
(London: Routledge, 2003 [1972]). For an Eastern Orthodox critique of the Papal claims see Philip Sherrard, *Church, Papacy and Schism: A Theological Enquiry*
(Limnia, Evia, Greece: Denise Harvey, 1996 [1976]).

7. Paul Tillich, *A History of Christian Thought* (New York, 1968), 51; Johannes Quasten, Patrology, 4 vols. (Utrecht and Antwerp: Spectrum Publishers; Westminster,
MD: Newman *Press and Christian Classics*, 1994), 4.342. Cited in Farrell, "Outline,"
unpaginated section headed "The Dialectical God of Augustinism and the Inver-
sion of the Patristic Ordo Theologiae."

8. On Augustine's equation of his theological first principle—the divine essence—with his philosophical first principle—the Plotinian One—see Farrell,
"Introduction."

the multiplicity of its Trinity of Persons, and this fact seems to disallow any true distinction between the divine attributes, the divine Persons, and the divine essence. Indeed, in the Augustino-Platonic scheme the divine essence came to have a status almost as a fourth Person of the Holy Trinity, as the Western *Scutum Fidei*, or "Shield of Faith," with its fourth central circle, often labeled "Deus," unwittingly indicates.

By the time of Philip the Fair's reign, both the Pope and the French king were locked in a fierce power struggle, and Farrell gives us some insight into why this clash was well nigh inevitable for the Augustinian West: A type of legal monophysitism had taken hold in the West according to which a new abstract "legal" conception of the office of Pope/king was set in opposition to the actual human being who held the office.[9] This bizarre formulation, the history of which is examined in Ernst Kantorowicz's *The King's Two Bodies*, is the end result of a long process of de-liturgization and de-concretization in Western political and religious culture. Ironically, Kantorowicz and Farrell point out, the Papacy was not immune to this de-liturgizing virus, but rather succumbed to it all too readily.[10] The main points to be kept in mind are that:

1. Augustine's Neoplatonic Trinity, with its precedent, utterly simple essence, led to

2. a new notion of King-Pope relations (based upon the abstractions of late medieval legal theory) which *a*) wrenched the Pope and the King from their original function as shepherds of the Truth, and *b*) focused solely on an absolute and absolutizing "Reason of State" to develop policy.

---

9. It is not being suggested that the West became Augustinian and then Francised in a preordained, deterministic manner. Rather, it is held that once Augustine became the highest authority in the West, and since the *Regnum Francorum* increasingly prominent as an Augustinian Christian Empire, these forces worked together to create the kind of sociopolitical climate conducive to "king's two bodies" monophysitism.

10. Kantorowicz, *King's Two Bodies*.

3. The new de-liturgized State, based on the new anhypostatic Law, found its analogue in the newly emerg-
ing Papal claims, the latter relying henceforth less and
less on adherence to the personal truth of "faith," and
turning more and more to "fidelity"—a new conception
of the Pope as the ultimate liege lord, a coercive power
having no conceivable limit. In such an Augustinized,
and thus Platonized, socio-religious milieu, the term
"Catholic" ceased to mean "according to the Truth," and
came to mean "submission to the authority of the Pope."

Doubtless the preceding summary of the convoluted path,
full of unlikely twists and breathtaking recapitulations, which
led from the Platonizing innovations of Augustine to the
earthshaking showdown between Philip the Fair and Boniface
VIII, raises as many questions as it answers. For further reading, consult Kantorowicz's previously mentioned *The King's
Two Bodies* and Joseph P. Farrell's *magnum opus: God, History
and Dialectic*.

It is now necessary to turn our attention to Philip the Fair.
The remainder of this section will attempt to trace the king's
inscrutable, contradictory, and often downright neurotic be-
havior to its root in the Western monophysitic theory of kingship. Our thesis is that Philip the Fair followed the theory of
the king's two bodies more self-consciously and more circum-
spectly than anyone, perhaps, who reigned before or after him.

Chapter Six

A Case of Arrested Thelemma: The King Strikes Back

To monarchize, be feared, and kill with looks
As if in the flesh which walls about our life,
were brass impregnable.
                    —William Shakespeare, *King Richard II*, III.ii, 165-168.[11]

B ishop Saisset, a man whose name is found in history books mainly because his enmity against Philip the Fair led to a notable phase in the investiture contest, is said to have spoken these rancorous words of the king: Philip the Fair is "neither man nor beast, but only image."[12] Playing upon Philip's epithet—"le Bel"—Saisset's words only grow more caustic: King Philip is "the handsomest of birds which is worth absolutely nothing...such is our king of France who is the handsomest man in the world and who can do nothing except to stare at men."[13] Many contemporaries shared Saisset's impression of the King's extreme passivity, a quality that Philip knowingly and artfully combined with an equally exaggerated sense of his royal majesty.[14] Philip's appearance in public often inspired an almost apocalyptic terror in his

11. Cited in Kantorowicz, *King's Two Bodies*, 30.
12. Cited in Elizabeth A. R. Brown, "Persona et Gesta: The Image and Deeds of the Thirteenth-Century Capetians. The Case of Philip the Fair." *Viator* 19 (1988): 219-246. Reproduced in *The Monarchy of Capetian France and Royal Ceremonial* (Aldershot: Variorum, 1991), VII, 228.
13. *Pierre Dupuy, Histoire du differend d'entre le pape Boniface VIII et Philippe le Bel...* (Paris, 1655), 643. Cited in Joseph R. Strayer, "Philip the Fair—A 'Constitutional' King," *American Historical Review* 62.1 (October, 1956): 18-32, at 19.
14. For a full discussion of Philip's statue-like demeanor see Jean Favier, *Philippe le Bel* (Paris: Librairie Arthme Fayard, 1978), 1-9.

subjects. At these well-staged events the king stood as a type of Stoic central point—or as the "unextended point" of hermeticism discussed elsewhere in this volume[15]—amidst his imposing entourage. Note this Englishman's reaction to the king's appearance at Vienne in 1311: "He comes with a host of people and [great] furor. We fear his raging and we tremble at his coming."[16] Doubtless Philip's "raging" was precisely his undemonstrative yet ultra-imperial manner. As Joseph R. Strayer epitomized Philip's royal persona, "he *was* the image on the great seal, enthroned alone in his royal glory."[17]

Yet, there is more to this picture, or to this statue, if you prefer. Many were not overawed by Philip the Fair's iconic pretensions, as evinced by the stream of criticism of the king that flowed more or less without refrain from the Pope's pen until Philip succeeded in installing his own more accommodating Pope, Clement V, who just happened to have been a Frenchman. Somewhat closer to home, Geffroi de Paris published a poem which dovetailed two insults against Philip by implying that the king was so silent and statue-like in public because during his incessant excursions in the royal forests he regularly ended the hunt with "the least" of the prey.[18] Indeed, Philip the Fair's carefully orchestrated projection of himself as royal icon *par excellence* had its flip-side, for the king showed his ire whenever he sensed that his royal will was opposed or his majestic dignity oppugned. On one occasion, the king "ordered submerged in the river with a stone attached to his neck a certain man who said that all the wine in Paris could not fill [the king] up. The king declared, 'I'll at least fill you up with water,' and the man drank on and on."[19] Let us keep this image

15. Andrew W. Lewis, *Royal Succession in Capetian France: Studies on Familial Order and the State* (Cambridge, MA and London: Harvard University Press, 1981), 148.

16. Cited from a dispatch of Henry Fykeis to the Bishop of Norwich published in Charles-Victor Langlois, "Notices et documents relatifs à l'histoire du XIIe et du XIVe sicle: Nova curie," *Revue historique* 87 (1905): 55-79, at 75. Langlois cited in Brown, "Persona et Gesta," 231.

17. Joseph R. Strayer, *The Reign of Philip the Fair* (Princeton, NJ: Princeton University Press, 1980), 12.

18. Lewis, *Royal Succession*, 148.

19. Brown, "Persona et Gesta," 230-231. Brown cites Paris, Bibliothèque nationale

of Philip as a cruel avenger of his own royal honor in mind as we turn back to the first side of the coin—Philip's career as a statue, a living icon of kingship.

The main historiographical problem of Philip the Fair scholarship is the question as to whether Philip actually *did* anything effectual during his reign or instead let his dynamic team of *über*-lawyers control royal policy, and it seems quite obvious that this interpretive quandary is not unrelated to the issue of the king's stoic persona. As Joseph Strayer commented, "it is hard to prove that any important act of the reign was the result of a personal decision by the king. *It is easy to argue that he did nothing.*"[20] However, Strayer's seminal *The Reign of Philip the Fair* paints quite a different picture of the king as regnally hyperactive, indeed almost frenetic in his scheming to expand royal prerogatives into new areas.[21]

At this point it is necessary to take a step back and make a stab at interpreting Philip the Fair's sphinx-like persona. Now, if we couple Strayer's thesis that Philip was both a statue in appearance and a dynamo in reality with Elizabeth Brown's well-grounded contention that Philip expended vast energies in trying to manage his public image, then it becomes clear why contention has always dogged attempts to interpret Philip's character, for Philip as king was *both* active *and* passive.[22]

MS lat. 541, fol. 75v.

20. Strayer, "'Constitutional' King," 18, emphasis added.

21. Strayer, Reign, x, xii-xiii. "Philip was the first French king to impose general taxes, and he was surprisingly successful in this innovation. His tax of 1304 produced more money than any tax levied during the next half century" (xii). The thelemic ambiguity that, it is here argued, causes so much interpretive difficulty as regards Philip's action or lack thereof, is reflected in the previously mentioned epithet "le bel." The Florentine Dominican Remigio de' Gerolami (d. 1319) preached a sermon that mentioned a "lady of Provence who called him dumb" (Trans. in D.L. D'Avray, *Death and the Prince: Memorial Preaching before 1350* [Oxford: Clarendon Press, 1994], 80). Whether or not this epithet was honorific in its original intent, it is clear that the Florentine preacher has interpreted it as such. It certainly could be argued that Philip, who viewed the leading families of the outlying lands of the Frankish kingdom with unbounded contempt and sometimes objectified these sentiments through his actions, was equally capable of inspiring either contempt (cf. Bsp. Saisset's comments) or incomprehension from his many auditors.

22. Brown, "Prince is Father," 313.

The paradox can be stated even more plainly: Philip's life was an active movement of inaction, a tragic quest for the nullification of human operations, a suppression of the merely human person. One virtue of our thesis that Philip the Fair's life was a case of arrested *thelema* is that it answers questions about the king that otherwise remain impenetrable. Take the following statement about Philip from Strayer: "There are almost no anecdotes about him…. (-) It is a great deal easier to think of Philip as a symbol of monarchy than to understand him as a man."[23] These chapters on King Philip propose that the issue that befuddled Strayer is a lot simpler than anyone has yet suspected: Philip the Fair of France wanted to *be* a true icon of the divine. From one angle, there is nothing noteworthy in Philip's deific aspiration, since the theory of kingship in the West is based upon the notion that the king is *christomimetes*, the only true wielder of divine grace.[24] However, viewed from another vantage point, that of the bizarre development in the West of the meaning of "icon" in the context of kingly ritual and dogma, Philip's desire to be one with the divine royal archetype shows itself to be a rather gothic *reductio ad absurdum*. It now becomes necessary to retrace our steps back to the early Visigothic and Frankish roots of royal religion in order to better understand what factors led to such an odd late medieval climax: the troubling spectacle of a king, the most powerful man in the world, who thinks he is a statue.

---

23. Strayer, *Reign*, 3.
24. Kantorowicz, *King's Two Bodies*, 47.

Chapter Seven

Political Theology East and West

From the fifth century to the eighth century, the decline of the Western half of the Roman Empire into a chaotic cultural backwater was accompanied by what has been described as the rise of Hellenistic monarchy in the Eastern part of the Empire, centered of course in Constantinople New Rome.[25] It is essential to note that in Eastern Roman society (and until the Carolingian period, Western Roman society as well), the *regnum* was thought of in terms of a cooperative relationship with the *sacerdotium*, that is, the Church and Her Patriarch. The development of the coronation ceremony, which became centered more and more on the ecclesial basis of kingly power though it retained the element of popular assent through acclamation, has been misinterpreted in Western scholarship as evidence either of "caesaropapism" or of an abiding "secular" element in the Eastern Roman conception of *imperium*.[26] A quotation from scholar Janet L. Nelson elucidates the profound differences between the Eastern Roman and the later Western conceptions of the *imperium*:

25. N.H. Baynes, "Eusebius and the Christian Empire," *Annuaire de l'institut de philology et d'histoire orientales* 2 (1933-1934): 13-18.

26. For a refutation of the West's notion of an Eastern Roman "caesaropapism," see Deno J. Geanakoplos, "Church and State in the Byzantine Empire: A Reconsideration of the Problem of Caesaropapism," in *Byzantine East and Latin West: Two Worlds of Christendom in Middle Ages and Renaissance: Studies in Ecclesiastical and Cultural History* (New York: Barnes and Noble, 1966), 55-83. Also see Geanakoplos's bibliography on "caesaropapism," ibid., 195-196. On the historiographical fiction of a secular Eastern Roman *imperium* see the comments and citations in Janet L. Nelson, "National Synods, Kingship as Office, and Royal Anointing: An Early Medieval Syndrome," in *Politics and Ritual in Early Medieval Europe* (London and Ronceverte: Hambledon Press, 1986), 239-281. Originally published in *Studies in Church History* 13 (1976): 97-119.

Of course, the clerical hierarchy existed as a specialist institution in eastern as in western christendom. But in Byzantium it produced no hierocratic theory, laid no claim to monopolise active participation in the church—which in a sociological sense was coterminous with the community of Christian believers. The divine will was believed to operate directly through all members of this community. Thus sixth-century theorists focussed [sic] not on the coronation…but on election and consent as the crucial elements in imperial inauguration. And in election and consent, leading officials, senators and people…are all involved in the expression of the divine choice, and precisely their coincidence generates a 'lawful succession' (*ennomos anarresis*). In such an inclusive cosmology, the patriarch took his place without friction alongside other channels of divine communication.[27]

In this conception of the emperor as fulfilling a divine ministry alongside the other ministries of "Church" and "people," there is no system of "checks and balances" rife with coercive tension as in modern "democracies" nor is there any idea of

27. Nelson, "Politics and Ritual," 267-268. Later in the same insightful article, Nelson further outlines the differences between Eastern and Western notions of *imperium*: "Where a western king prostrated himself before his inauguration a Byzantine emperor remained standing throughout his acclamation and coronation alike. Thus the coronation, unlike the western anointing, effected no symbolic rebirth, was not dynamic: it was a static representation of a pre-existing fact, an articulated icon. (-) Hence the exercise of full governmental powers by a 'new' emperor during the time-lag between anagoreusis and coronation; and hence also, I suggest, the absence in Byzantium of anything equivalent to the western 'coronation' oath. (-) The Byzantine inauguration ritual was never devised and managed exclusively by clerics. Its details were revised by the emperors themselves, according to Constantine Porphyrogenitus, 'in whatever way each thinks fit'" (271-272). As opposed to the *Regnum Francorum*, which was tension-ridden owing to its racial/economic divide between Franks (free nobles) and villains (unfree, non-Frankish serfs), the Eastern Roman Empire saw the entire society of persons as anointed, not just the higher clergy and the king, as in Frankish Civilization: "Conversely, [in the East,] the anointed, the Christian Romans, formed a single community, within which the emphasis was not on boundaries but on communications. Characteristic of Byzantine society were rituals of mass participation: the processions of the emperor or of relics or images through the great cities, the adventus, the acclamations in the vernacular of the crowds in the hippodromes, and in the great churches the elaborate preparation of chrism by the patriarch 'before all the people.' To the pure, all things are holy" (276).

an autocratic secular ruler who mediates literally between God and Law, as in the later developments of the medieval West.[28] Instead, there is a *symphonia* between the emperor, the Church, and the people, a harmonization of purpose based upon the Orthodoxy of each individual within each tangential sphere. The purity of Chalcedonian Orthodoxy was the basis of all politics, art, and wisdom in the Eastern Roman Empire, because the purity of belief undergirt the proper fulfilling of each charismatic ministry, from the lowliest farmer to the emperor himself. Some may try to refute this notion of an Eastern Roman Orthodox *symphonia* as a hopelessly idealistic notion that never actually existed in practice. However, just as the notion of a capitalist free market (or a pre-capitalist free market) is based largely upon negations—such as the absence of centralized planning, etc.—which are not absolute but rather indications of aspiration and purpose, so the Orthodox *symphonia* consists in apophatic principles which gesture toward the correlating ministries of emperor, Church, and people without a cataphatic, positive, and therefore legalistic definition of absolute vectors of power.[29] Because of its basis in Orthodox

---

28. For the king as a mediator of God and Law see Kantorowicz, *King's Two Bodies*, 87-192.

29. Fr. John Meyendorff, in his *Imperial Unity and Christian Divisions* (Crestwood, NY: St. Vladimir's Orthodox Seminary Press, 1989), provides a more than adequate presentation and analysis of the Orthodox Roman concept of "symphonia":

> In Justinian's view, the issue was not—as it is for us—in defining relations between 'Church and 'State,' as two distinct social structures. For Justinian, in terms of geographical extension, general goals and membership, the two coincided. God's will was to unite the 'inhabited earth'...under Himself, as Creator and Savior. The Christian Roman emperor was entrusted with this task and in this sense he was accomplishing on earth the ministry of Christ himself. The Church, however, was to realize sacramentally that which was implied by the Christian faith. The people of God were therefore to be led by two distinct hierarchies: the one, responsible for external order, welfare, security and administration, and the other leading the people of God into the sacramental anticipation of the Kingdom of God. Their competencies were, therefore, distinct, but inseparable. Their activities and practical responsibilities necessarily overlapped. The bishops presided over the Eucharist and taught the faith, but the emperor alone could provide them with

apophasis, the Eastern Romans refused to place ultimate authority in any external body *per sé*, even that of an Ecumenical Council. This is why Westerners, who know only *cataphasis* in politics and faith, and who thus can point to neat, absolute structures of power, which they mistakenly equate with good order or "rational governance," see nothing but confusion and disorder in an East Roman society that refuses to accept the many varieties of feudalistic oppression which have developed in the West, instead following the original *politeia* of Christian Hellenism. This Orthodox view of politics sees society as the coming together of the people of God in an ascetic, communal "work of the people" (*leitourgeia*) which accepts no final authority save that based in communion with God. Needless to say, the divine-human communion of the Eastern Roman

---

the means of getting together, of enjoying enough 'good order' to be able to exercise their ministry properly....

The most famous text issued by Justinian on this subject is his *Novella 6*, a "new" law, to be added to the *Code*.... In the preamble to the *Novella*, the emperor defines a formal ideological principle:

"There are two great gifts which God, in his love for man, has granted from on high: the priesthood...and the imperial dignity (*Basileia*). The first serves divine things, while the latter directs and administers human affairs; both, however, proceed from the same origin and adorn the life of mankind. Hence, nothing should be such a source of care to the emperors as the dignity of the priests, since it is for their (imperial) welfare that they constantly implore God. For if the priesthood is in every way free from blame and possesses access to God, and if the emperors administer equitably and judiciously the state entrusted to their care, general harmony (*symphonia tis agathe*) will result and whatever is beneficial will be bestowed upon the human race."

What Justinian obviously could not—or would not—define is how harmony or 'symphony' was to be established between the eschatological reality of the Kingdom of God, manifested in the Church and its sacraments, on the one hand, and, on the other, such 'human affairs,' inevitable in any society, as violence, war, social injustice, etc., which the state by itself is neither capable, no willing to avoid. Therefore, the preamble of the Sixth Novella describes nothing but an aspiration (208-210. cited in Farrell, *Outline*, section entitled "God, History, and Dialectic: Explorations of the Philosophical and Theological Foundations of the Two Europes," v-vi).

society is opposed to that of the supposedly divine princes of the West, who have become deified through their anointing with uncreated Holy Oil and/or through the simple fact that they have blue Frankish blood in their veins.[30] Rather, the Orthodox society places all hope in *theosis*, the union with the energies of the Holy Trinity achieved by prophets, apostles and saints, some of whom have been emperors, farmers, soldiers, and Patriarchs.

In the cataphatic formulation of Western or Frankish Civilization, sacred kings and imperial bishops—each enthroned on one side of a dialectically opposed, divinely constituted binary of power—locked horns in the notorious Investiture Contest.[31] To skip ahead for a moment, let us not forget that Philip the Fair's kidnapping and mauling of Pope Boniface VIII through the offices of William of Nogaret is the last pathetic scene in the drama of Investiture.[32] No equivalent to the sorry spectacle of Investiture ever did, nor ever could transpire in the Eastern Roman Empire, for there was no Frankish Civilization (feudalism) in the East, until rapacious Frankish crusaders brought it there in the thirteenth century, perpetrating unspeakable outrages against the Orthodox Romans they tried to enslave there.[33] Needless to say, wherever and whenever the Franks were ousted, it was a simultaneous eradication of feudal institutions and feudal law.

---

30. For the origin of the Frankish Holy Ampoule and its oil, see Sergio Bertelli, *The King's Body: Sacred Rituals of Power in Medieval and Early Modern Europe*, trans. R. Burr Litchfield (University Park, PA: Pennsylvania State University Press, 2001 [1990]), 25-26. The Frankish kings believed that they, and they alone, could be referred to as "Most Christian King," on the basis of their exclusive access to the oil of the Ampoule. For a full exposition of the notion of "Most Christian King," which also analyses Frankish royal religion in general, see Jean de Pange, *Le Roi Très Chrétien* (Paris: Librairie Arthème Fayard, 1949).
31. On investiture see U.-R. Blumenthal, *The Investiture Controversy: Church and Monarchy from the Ninth to the Twelfth Century* (Philadelphia, 1988).
32. For a narrative account of Nogaret's abduction of Pope Boniface VIII at Agnani, see T.S.R. Boase, *Boniface VIII* (London: Constable and Co., 1933), 344-351.
33. For an analysis of Frankish feudalism and the attempt to force it on the Eastern Roman Empire see Ernst H. Kantorowicz, "'Feudalism' in the Byzantine Empire," in *Feudalism in History*, ed. Rushton Coulborn (Hamden, CT: Archon Books, 1965), 151-166. On the Fourth Crusade of 1204 see Papadakis and Meyendorff, 199-238.

Now we will follow this excursus into medieval history with a concluding section. Because of the enigmatic nature of Philip's personality, which has caused all scholars until now to, in one way or another, throw up their hands in despair, we will try to draw everything together in a perhaps risky but undoubtedly courageous closing discourse. Do not be surprised to find yourself asked to squint at grainy illustrations or to agree to seemingly inordinate leaps of thought. It is high time that the spirit of Frances Yates was conjured forth to confront the ghost of King Philip. Why? Because the issue of Philip the Fair's dilemma of will, like the issue of the origin and nature of alchemy covered in Part 1, has refused to yield any satisfying answers when approached through the heretofore "accepted" means of scholarly analysis. It is time to gently push the envelope, hoping against hope that it does not tear in half.

Conclusion

Philip's "regis inordinate voluntas"[34]

T he preceding chapters of this, our study's second part, have aimed to show that Philip the Fair's case of arrested *thelema*, far from being a Frankish version of Roman decadence, is rather the logical (or illogical) conclusion to a specifically Frankish course of development. It is in the history of what Ernst Kantorowicz called "mediaeval political theology" that we find plausible antecedents for Philip's ambivalence toward the exertion of his royal will. First we will outline Kantorowicz's insightful view that an Augustinian monophysitism was operative in the peculiar course of Western legal theory that led to Philip's complex. Next we will undertake a brief re-examination of some aspects of Philip the Fair's character, this time focusing on the specific Kantorowiczian "king's two bodies" thesis, drawing conclusions and expansions that suggest themselves along the way.

Ernst Kantorowicz is not the only scholar to note that both Continental and English traditions of medieval law were at least as dependent upon Chalcedonian Christological formulations as they were on any other written source, even Roman Law; but, he *was* the first to see their origin in Blessed Augustine's theology and he was the first to draw far-reaching conclusions from this connection. Kantorowicz starts off in Medieval England, from whence he quotes Edmund Plowden's *Reports* as saying

> the King has in him two Bodies, *viz.*, a Body natural, and a Body politic. His Body natural...is...subject to all

---

34. John of Hoscem, canon of Liege, in 1334 wrote that Philip's overbearing will, his "regis inordinate voluntas," was responsible for the Templar dissolution (J.N. Hillgarth, *Ramon Lull and Lullism in Fourteenth-Century France* [Oxford: Clarendon Press, 1971], 91).

Infirmities.... (-) But his body politic is a Body that cannot be seen or handled...and this Body is utterly void of Infancy, and old Age, and other natural Defects and Imbecilities...and for this Cause, what the King does in his Body politic, cannot be invalidated or frustrated by an Disability in his natural Body.[35]

John Fortescue is quoted by Kantorowicz as having the same notion of the king's *character angelicus*: The king's heavenly body politic, though Plowden claims it cannot be touched, turns out to be "Immutable within Time," and thus incapable of error in concrete, temporal matters.[36] Many other political theorists of the day developed further the parallel between the Chalcedonian dogma of Christ's two natures—one divine, one human, but both in one divine Hypostasis—and the notion of the king's two bodies. The Norman Anonymous proclaimed that the king was

a *twin person*, one descending from nature, the other from grace.... One through which...he conformed with other men: another through which, by the eminence of [his] deification and by the power of the sacrament [of consecration], he excelled all others. Concerning one personality, he was, by nature, an individual man: concerning his other personality, he was, by grace, a *Christus*, that is, a God-man.[37]

Kantorowicz goes on to show that the Norman Anonymous's most likely source for his double hypostasis Christology with its concomitant royal "twinship" was the Toledan Councils of the sixth century. To the same locale and time (sixth century Spain) we can date the insertion of the *filioque* clause into the Nicene Creed and the rise of Adoptionism.[38] This constitutes a

35. Kantorowicz, King's Two Bodies, 7, citing Edmund Plowden, *Commentaries, or Reports of Edmund Plowden* (London: S. Brooke, Paternoster Row, 1816 [1571]), 212a.
36. Ibid., 8.
37. Ibid., 46, citing G.H. Pertz, ed., *Monumenta Germaniae Historica. Libelli de lite imperatorum et pontificum* (cited hereafter as MGH), 3.664.
38. Ibid., 51. On the origins of the *filioque* interpolation and the Toledan councils, see Richard S. Haugh, *Photius and the Carolingians: The Trinitarian Controversy*

direct line of influence from Adoptionism (which is Nestorian in its belief in a Christ from above which gradually comes to rest in the human body of Jesus) to the Norman Anonymous's equally Nestorian "twin person" of Christ. Most shocking about the Anonymous's Christology is its notion that the humanity of Christ is so separate from the divine nature that this human Christ must by all rights submit to the imperial office, since the latter is identified with the essence of Divine Justice: "It is as though the *potestas* of Tiberius *qua* Caesar were 'haloed,' whereas Christ, in his human serfdom, remains without halo."[39]

The Anonymous's extreme Nestorianism was indeed the proximal source for the idea of the king's two bodies in Plowden and all of the other legal theorists cited by Kantorowicz; however, the German-born medievalist is not slow to point to the Anonymous's precursors. Kantorowicz is amazed particularly at the frontispiece of the Aachen Gospels (ca. 975, fig. 7, page 161) that goes far beyond the Carolingian conventions toward which it nods. Holy Roman Emperor Otto is seated on a Carolingian-style throne, and he and his royal *cathedra* are depicted as being suspended in midair, the personification of earth, *Tellus*, performing the Atlas-like duty of shouldering throne and Emperor. The Emperor is presented as *christomimetes*—he who acts as Christ, or he who mimics Christ—and another detail tips off the deeper meaning of the Aachen miniature: "the divine aureola framing the Hand of God [that rests upon Otto's head] intersects with the imperial aureola, thus allowing the emperor's head to be placed in the spandrel which is formed by the intersecting haloes."[40] Surely, this inter-halo tangent is the inspiration for (or at least it constitutes an early corroboration of) the Norman Anonymous's notion of the king who has been "elevated even unto heaven.... (-) Truly, unto God he has been elevated...".[41] The mandorla of Christ, the four iconic animals representing the Four Gos-

(Belmont, MA: Nordland, 1975), 26-29.

39. Ibid., 54.

40. Ibid., 62.

41. Ibid., 63. Citation from MGH, 3.676, 5ff.

pels, the intersection of the Hand of God sphere and the Emperor's head—it is important to note along with Kantorowicz that these details are alterations of the traditional iconographic representations of emperors in the Eastern *and* Western Roman Empires. Specifically, the Frankish commentators and artists we have mentioned—from the Aachen artist who produced the Codex in the tenth century to the Norman Anonymous at the beginning of the twelfth century (along with the inheritors of this tradition in modern times)—have changed the Chalcedonian Orthodox representation of Christ, which proclaimed that Christ was one person in two natures, meaning that man becomes united with Christ by grace or energy, the Son of God being the only Son of the Father by nature. The Nestorianism of the king's two bodies says that the king has a physical body *and* a kingly body (the separation being stressed so absolutely as to include a bifurcated personality), and that the former may exhibit every weakness and shortcoming, but that the completely separate divine royal person remains perfect in justice and truth. Indeed, the sources cited above indicate that *the king's divine person was Christ by nature.*

Kantorowicz is not satisfied with these later interconnections, but proceeds to peel back yet another layer, which reveals Blessed Augustine of Hippo. Augustine's *Enarrationes in Psalmos*, a commentary on Psalm 91 that became a foundational ecclesiastical text in the Christian West, contains many passages that one might say constitute a programme for Nestorian theory of kingship, most notably the following cluster of passages: "In this very tabernacle the emperor has militated for us. (-) He is far above all heavens, but his feet he has on earth. (-) But we should not believe that the head is separate from the body: there is a discretion in space, but a conjunction in love."[42] It is remarkable enough that these passages seem to be the main inspiration for the king's two bodies theme in Western Imperial iconography. Here Joseph P. Farrell provides

---

42. Augustine, *Enarrationes in Psalmos*, 61.11; J.-P. Migne, ed., *Patrologia Latino*, 221 vols. (Paris, 1844-55), 37.1178. Cited in Kantorowicz, King's *Two Bodies*, 71-72.

the deeper insight to Kantorowicz's citation (though we cannot rule out that the myriad-minded German was aware of it
as well) by pointing out that Augustine's term "conjunction" is
the same term used by Nestorius and many of his followers to
indicate the nature of the contractual union between the human nature of Christ and His divine nature.[43]

Augustine did explicitly state that the word "tabernacle"
was used in the 91st Psalm to indicate the flesh of Christ.
However, later iconographers and ecclesiastical writers in
the West tended to use some of Augustine's unfortunate word
choices (as we noted above with "conjunction") as well as
the ambiguity of his formulations of Christological dogma,
despite the African bishop's Orthodox intentions. Icons informed by this Nestorianizing tradition of the disappearing
Christ do not picture the entire body of Jesus Christ; only
His feet are shown, the rest of Him being lost behind a cloud
border that has replaced the flesh of Christ as the newly conceived "tabernacle."[44]

Now, to move the action ahead to the time of King Philip
IV, let us note that Giles of Rome, a man who had the ear of
the king, wrote the following in a work dedicated to Philip: "...
[T]he king or prince is a kind of Law, and the Law is a kind
of king or prince. For the Law is a kind of inanimate prince;
the prince, however, a kind of animate Law. And in so far as
the animate exceeds the inanimate the king or prince must exceed the Law."[45] Couple this notion of a king as a literal em-
bodiment of an abstraction, Law, with another of Giles's ad-
monitions to Philip: "...[I]t is altogether fitting that kings and
princes exhibit themselves less than others and demonstrate
that they are graver and more worthy of reverence than others,
not for the sake of ostentation, but rather lest the royal dignity

---

43. See Farrell's *God, History and Dialectic*. Nestorius's word for "conjunction" was
συνάφεια.
44. Kantorowicz, *King's Two Bodies*, 73-74.
45. Giles of Rome, *De regimine principum* in R.W. and A.J. Carlyle, *A History of Mediaeval Political Theory in the West*, 6 vols. (Edinburgh and London: William Blackwood and Sons Ltd., 1903-1936), 5.75. Cited in Kantorowicz, *King's Two Bodies*,
134.

be scorned."[46] Giles above all counseled Philip not to appear "severe but rather deserving of veneration."[47] Giles's advice to Philip was a distillation and development of Nestorianizing notions about the proper nature of the *imperium*.

Another area where the connection is palpable between the Nestorianizing notion of the king's two bodies and Philip the Fair is in the king's regnal seals. Philip's great seal, shown to the right of Philip's father's seal in figure 8 (page 162), shows Philip the Fair's head poking through the outer rim of the seal. Notice that Philip III's seal also features the conventional Ottonian depiction of the royal head breaking out of the border, but Philip III's expanding head is outdone by Philip IV's, whose crown breaks not only the inner but also the outer rim of the seal. Elizabeth Brown notes the less wolfish and more imposing lions that flank the larger seal, and she also sets up our comparison with a similar seal of Philip's:

> Further, on Philip the Fair's great seal the four richly maned lions' heads adorning the throne are clearly distinguishable from the long-necked wolf-like creatures portrayed on his father's seal. It is doubtless no coincidence that the lion also appeared on Philip the Fair's secret seal. The king of beasts, identified with Jesus Christ, the symbol of magnanimity as well as vigilance and retributive justice, was a fitting sign for Philip himself; he was surely aware of the lion's attributes when he chose to associate it so prominently with himself.[48]

The secret seal of Philip the Fair (fig. 9, page 162) to which Brown alludes is not only noteworthy because dominated by the lion image, but also because of its triadic shape. Specifically, the seal is in the shape of three interlocking rings, each ring containing its own triple ring that mirrors the larger trine. If we hearken back to our foregoing discussion of the *Scutum*

---

46. Giles of Rome, *De Regimine principum libri III* (Rome: Stephan Plannck, 1482), 2.3.19.
47. Cited in Brown, "Persona et Gesta," 232.
48. Ibid., 222.

fidei and its filioquist trinitarian undergirding, interesting thought-vistas open. Figure 2 (page 158) shows the double shield of faith, one representing the Holy Trinity, the other representing the parts of the human soul. Figure 6 (page (160) shows a triple representation in that the *Scutum* containing the Father, Son and Holy Spirit stands beside an alchemical vessel with a white, a blue, and a red phoenix, which together form an Ouroboros. Thus, figure 6 weds the spatial trinity of three Persons to a diachronic trinity that is identified with the alchemical Great Work. In Philip the Fair's secret seal we find a *Scutum*-style configuration of three trinities, which, each trine taken as ring in the meta-structure, forms a larger trinity. The seal links this process-*Scutum* with a single image that threatens to envelop the entire surface of the image, a royal lion. It seems that this lion, representing at once both Jesus Christ and the Frankish king, is parallel logically and iconographically to the utterly simple divine essence of the *Scutum fidei, le point parfait* marked "Deus." We will now leave the curious subject of Philip the Fair's personality with the following conclusion, which, it is hoped, speaks beyond its immediate application by drawing together the individual filaments that, taken together, make up the cloth of this chapter: *If Philip the Fair indeed saw himself as the divine lion that is both the radically simple divine essence and the process of divine development, then his neurosis has a theological counterpart in the Western trinitarian confusion of essence, energy and person.*

3

"Scientia Generalis": The Ecumenical Task of Natural Philosophy According to G.W. Leibniz

"By understanding the laws of the mechanisms of divine invention, we shall perfect ourselves far more than by merely following the constructions accepted by men. For what greater master can we find than God, the author of the universe? And what more beautiful hymn can we sing to him than one in which the witness of things themselves expresses his praise?"

G W .L eibniz' An Introduction on the Value and Method of Natural Science"[1]

1   Leroy E. Loemaker, ed., *Gottried Wilhelm Leibniz: Philosophical Papers and Letters, 2 vols.* (Chicago: University of Chicago Press, 1956), 1.432. [Hereafter cited as LL.]

GODEFROI GUILLAUME LEIBNITZ

Il fut dans l'Univers connu par ses Ouvrages,
Et dans son Païs même, il se fit respecter:
Il instruisit les Rois, il éclaira les Sages,
Plus sage qu'eux il sut douter.

VOLTAIRE.

Chapter Eight

G.W. Leibniz: Life and Character

Biographical Introduction

Gottfried Wilhelm Leibniz, one of Germany's most influential philosophers, was born on 1 July 1646 in Leipzig. As a youth he read widely in virtually every area of study, then took degrees in philosophy and law before traveling widely and, after many twists and turns, ending up as head librarian at the Court of Hanover under Duke Johann Friedrich (1625-1679). Before he died in 1716, Leibniz published several groundbreaking treatises in the fields of law, mathematics, theology, philosophy, and physics. He created the first calculating machine that could perform all of the operations of basic arithmetic and he, independent of Sir Isaac Newton, discovered the laws of integral and differential calculus.[1]

Since space permits only a brief look at Leibniz's work, the following statements on the philosopher's background and influences will be selective. Leibniz attempts to construct an all-inclusive, encyclopedic system of knowledge to both 1) establish the rational basis of all the sciences *and* 2) provide reasonable proofs for the dogmas of Christianity. He starts by asking questions about the nature of knowledge itself: How can one arrive at truth, and what is the proper method for accepting rationally presented arguments? Once this method is established, Leibniz reasons, it should be applied to two areas, 1) the material realm of bodies—this is the world of science or natural philosophy—and

---

1. On Leibniz's invention (or co-invention with Sir Isaac Newton) of the infinitesimal calculus see Jason Socrates Bardi, *The Calculus Wars: Newton, Leibniz, and the Greatest Mathematical Clash of All Time* (New York: Thunder's Mouth Press, 2006).

2) the world behind materiality—the spiritual world of monads. These realms—the physical and the metaphysical—can only be harmonized through the right philosophical method. Thus theory and praxis are bound together by Leibniz's ecumenism, which is a *rationaliste procedure par excellence*. This essay aims to show that Leibniz's ecumenism, far from being only a religious quest, rather is rooted in his universal philosophical method. As Nicholas Jolley concludes, "[i]t is not inappropriate, then, to seek to explain Leibniz's enthusiasm for the project of ecumenism [merely] in terms of his deep metaphysical commitments."[2] The grandiosity of Leibniz's cosmic ecumenism was certainly not unique in the world of seventeenth century thought, nor was his emphasis on a simple repeatable mental procedure that promised an amazing cure of social and spiritual ills. Leibniz lived in the shadow of a group of irenicist Christian philosophers known as the Herborn encyclopedists—amongst them John Amos Comenius and Johann Heinrich Alsted—who exhibited great enthusiasm for simple pedagogical techniques believed to be gateways to a society completely free of social ills.[3] The following analysis

2. Nicholas Jolley, "Leibniz, Locke, and the Epistemology of Toleration," in *Leibniz and the English-Speaking World*, ed. Pauline Phemister and Stuart C. Brown (Dordrecht, Netherlands: Springer, 2007), 133-143, at 143.

3. See Leroy E. Loemaker, "Leibniz and the Herborn Encyclopedists," *Journal of the History of Ideas* 22.3 (July-Sept 1961), 323-338. On Comenius's theology of conversion, see Howard Louthan, "Introduction," in *John Comenius: The Labyrinth of the World and the Paradise of the Heart* (Mahwah, NJ: Paulist Press, 1998), 7-54, where Louthan, esp. p. 19ff., outlines Comenius's "pansophism" as it relates to Comenius's scheme of universal Christian education. In short, Comenius believed that Roman Catholic Christianity was corrupted through the scholastic system of abstract concepts. This scholastic system of dialectical concepts was the antithesis of Adamic "naming." Comenius sought to reestablish pure Adamic pedagogy through simple moral lessons linked to picture games that he believed built literal, empirical bridges between *words*, on one hand; and *objects and processes in nature*, on the other. According to Comenius, these "picture games," with their Pietistic moral lessons gleaned from simple observations of the senses, revealed the unitary wisdom of God, to which all would submit if they followed the Comenian pedagogy. In *Occult America: The Secret History of How Mysticism Shaped Our Nation* (New York: Bantam, 2009), Mitch Horowitz looks into the continuing influence of *rationaliste procedure* mysticism on American civil religion in the Gilded Age and beyond. See pp. 80-99. A good example of the rationaliste procedure theology in the United States is Disciple of Christ Walter Scott's (1796-1861) revivalism. Scott's program "had six points: faith, repentance, baptism, remission of sins, gift of the Holy Spirit, and life eter-

of Leibniz aims to show that the great German polymath's cosmic ecumenism was more than just a compartment of his thought. Rather, an understanding of his ecumenism shows how Leibniz can be both extremely abstract and at the same time eminently practical in his various international schemes and in his philosophy.[4] Much like Plato, who in the *Laws* outlined his vision of an ideal polis, all the while realizing tacitly that "[t]his blueprint as a whole [was] never likely to find such favorable circumstances that every single detail [would] turn out precisely according to plan," Leibniz's overall goal of uniting God and creation in such a way that all created beings find perfection and happiness in the essence of God, could be spoken of *both* in terms of the ultimate telos *and also* in terms of institutional compromise.[5] To state things plainly, it is one and the same Leibniz who composed the inscrutable abstractions of *Monadology* and who wrote painstakingly detailed expositions on proper procedures and protocol at ecumenical conferences.

Overview of Leibnizian Thought

The Germany of Leibniz's youth reeled in the aftermath of the Thirty Years War (1618-1648), an ordeal of unprecedented devastation that killed an estimated one third of the

---

nal. To make them even simpler, the last two were combined, and the whole scheme reduced to a 'five-finger exercise' which could be comprehended even by children," in Sydney E. Ahlstrom, *A Religious History of the American People*, 2nd ed. (New Haven and London: Yale University Press, 2004 [1972]), 450. Note that Scott explained the necessity of baptism as having a *purely logical character*, being the natural conclusion that follows unavoidably from faith in Christ!

On the epistemological side of things: Alstead called his Augustino-Platonic theory of knowledge a "circle of the universe" which starts from logical first principles, descends in a Baconian manner to particulars, then "ascends from sense and singular things to universals; the resulting circular motion [being] perfection" (Loemaker, "Herborn," 326). Alstead's process is based in the same kind of logico-metaphysical dialectic that is in its main points identical to Leibniz's theory of knowledge in each of its phases.

4. One scholar who has perceived this interpretive problem and has proposed a solution to it based upon Leibniz's ecumenism is Txetxu Ausín. See items in bibliography.

5. Plato, *Laws* 5.745e-746a, translation by Trevor J. Saunders in *Plato: Complete Works*, Ed. John M. Cooper (Indianapolis, IN: Hackett, 1997), 1426.

population. The Thirty Years War was in great measure caused by the religious factionalism of the Protestant Reformation, and this fact ensured that religious unification and religious toleration would remain the most urgent international policy issues during these years. The social upheaval and religious splintering of the Reformation and its attendant wars left Europe in shock; many philosophers and theologians became millenarians or at the very least began to think more holistically. Social strife, a larger-than-life problem, could only be met with larger than life solutions, or so many believed. Some set about with gusto imagining all-inclusive categories and their syntheses, anything to encourage the hope that the unmanageable chaos around them could be corralled into neat, circumscribable wholes. Leibniz, born into a devout Lutheran family that had also known success in the academic world, viewed theology, philosophy and politics as aspects of the same scientific quest.[6] Faith and reason, many encyclopedists and holists believed, could heal all societal and confessional divisions and allow the attainment of the greatest good for all human beings.

---

6. Nicholas Jolley notes that Leibniz referred to his Church not as "Lutheran" but rather "Evangelical" (Jolley, "Leibniz, Locke," 134). From the Reformation era until today, many commonly referred to as Lutherans have preferred the less sectarian *Evangelisch*, esp. as the Church in Germany has been named officially *Deutsche Evangelische Kirche* since 1933, In 1817, Frederick William III of Prussia, wishing to end the conflict between Lutherans and Reformed in his kingdom, forcibly united them under a single name—Evengelical Church of the Prussian Union. For background see William Benton, "Lutheran Churches," in *The New Encyclopaedia Britannica in Thirty Volumes*, 15th ed. 11.198.

Chapter Nine

The Development of Leibniz's Science: From Hobbes' "Conatus" to the *Monadology*

Leibniz On the Motion of Bodies and the Motion Caused by Souls

Recent writing about the scientific revolution is stamping out the myth that the seventeenth century saw the overthrow of Aristotle and Scholasticism in the name of the so-called "mechanical philosophy."[7] In reality, many scientists

7. See John Henry, "Atomism and Eschatology: Catholicism and Natural Philosophy in the Interregnum," *British Journal for the History of Science* 15.3 (1982), 211-239. Though the main thrust of his argument pertains to the "Merton thesis"‡ about the Puritan origins of the "new philosophy," Henry also seeks to show the complex and reciprocal relationship between scholasticism and seventeenth century science. Most pertinent for our purposes is Henry's point that Catholic thinkers like Sir Kenelm Digby and Fr. Thomas White developed Aristotelian philosophical systems that were *both* atomistic *and* mechanical (213)! Leibniz was influenced by Digby and White, as noted by Nicholas Jolley (*The Cambridge Companion to Leibniz*, ed. N. Jolley, 64). Henry's notion of a continuing reliance on Aristotle in the scientific revolution is paralleled by Brian P. Copenhaver in "Did Science Have a Renaissance?," *Isis* 83.3 (1992): 387-407, wherein it is shown that before natural philosophy could do science with "the philosopher," Renaissance humanists were using the same Aristotelian corpus to support their disparate types of natural (and unnatural!) magic (403-406). Copenhaver does a superlative job in explicating the connection between Aristotelian philosophy and the Renaissance belief in an original linguistic transparence. The latter amounted to a hermetic Eunomianism that led its proponents to ferret out ancient manuscripts in the hopes of unearthing a purer language, one that had divine, Edenic power (406).

‡ *The "Merton thesis."* In 1938 Robert K. Merton published *Science, Technology and Society in Seventeenth-Century England* (New York: Harper and Row, 1970; orig. pub. *Osiris* 4.2 [1938]: 414-565), which caused great controversy with its assertion that a Puritan ethic of God-directed, utilitarian empiricism, with a

and philosophers who were in the vanguard of the new science were also followers of Aristotle and even of Aquinas. Leibniz, for instance, drank deep draughts of Scholastic theology at the University of Leipzig under his teacher Jakob Thomasius (1622-1684), who was nearly prevailed upon by his precocious student to support the reconciliation of the hidebound Aristotelianism of the schools with the modern philosophy of Descartes, Hobbes, and Gassendi.[8]

In fact, Leibniz, far from being unique in his enthusiasm, was rather following a tradition of Aristotelian/modern science previously established by thinkers like Sir Kenelm Digby and Thomas Hobbes, a tradition that sought to take what was true and lasting in Aristotle and to reconcile it with the newly discovered mechanical philosophy. Next we will spend a few pages examining Leibniz's critique of Cartesian matter theory, all the while relating its features to our present theme.

***   ***   ***

For Descartes and many of his followers, matter was equivalent to extension.[9] Essentially, they asserted that extension in space is the only property of bodies. Leibniz, reacting strongly against this Cartesian picture, proposed the following chain of propositions: 1) Things that are extended have parts and are thus divisible. 2) The ultimate base or bases of reality must be utterly simple, or else there is some thing that is simpler of which

---

concomitant indifference toward medieval scholasticism and its web of rules and definitions, accounted for the great number of Englishmen who excelled in natural philosophy during the 1600s. For a survey of the literature critical of Merton see H. Floris Cohen, *The Scientific Revolution: A Historiographical Inquiry* (Chicago and London: University of Chicago Press, 1994), 317-321.

8. On Thomasius see Stuart Brown and N.J. Fox, *Historical Dictionary of Leibniz's Philosophy* (Lanham, MD: The Scarecrow Press, Inc., 2006), 228-229. During his school days, Leibniz "read [the scholastics] more immoderately and eagerly than my teachers approved" (G.W. Leibniz, *Samtliche Schriften und Briefe*, ed. Academy of Sciences of Berlin, Series I-VIII [Darmstadt, Leipzig, and Berlin, 1923-], 2.1.401. Henceforth cited as DA. Orig. cit. Stuart Brown, "Leibniz's Formative Years [1646-76]: An Overview," in *The Young Leibniz and His Philosophy* [1646-76], ed. Stuart Brown [Dordrecht: Kluwer, 1999], 1-18, at 3).

9. Rene Descartes, *The Philosophical Writings of Descartes*, 3 vols, trans. J. Cottingham, R. Stoothoff, D. Murdoch, and A. Kenney (Cambridge, 1984-1991), 1.53.

the former are composed.[10] 3) Therefore, extension is accidental, and pertains not to essence.[11] An essence, according to Leibniz, must be a non-extended, totally simple unit, or "monad."[12] In order to better understand the reasons for and development of his critique of atomism and extension matter theory, we will now reproduce a few of Leibniz's own words on the subject:

> At first, after freeing myself from bondage to Aristotle, I accepted the void and the atoms, for it is these that best satisfy the imagination. But, in turning back to them after much thought, I perceived that it is impossible to find the principles of a true unity in matter alone or in what is merely passive, since everything in it is but a collection or aggregation of parts to infinity. Now a multitude can derive its reality only from the *true unities*, which have some other origin are entirely different from points. To find these real unities, therefore, I was forced to have recourse to a *formal atom, since a material being cannot be at the same time material and perfectly indivisible, or endowed with true unity.*[13]

Here the atom's extension in space is shown by Leibniz to offer no satisfactory answer to the question "what is the ground of unity which holds atoms together?" Leibniz, more apt to use good arguments from the past than to make up new ones, returns to the scholastic definition of *substantia* in his critique of the Cartesian *res extensa*.[14] He rejects the Cartesian definition of the essence of matter as *extension* and *qualities*, for these two categories do not in any way account for how

10. *G.W. Leibniz: Philosophical Texts*, trans. Richard Francks and R.S. Woolhouse (Oxford: Oxford University Press, 1998), 268. [Hereafter cited as PT.] See the same passage as trans. by P. Wiener in *Leibniz: Selections* (New York: Charles Scribner's Sons, 1951), 533: "And there must be simple substances, since there are composites; for the composite is only a collection or aggregatum of simple substances." See also DA 6.98.
11. DA 6.1.533.
12. From the Greek "monas," or "unit."
13. G.W. Leibniz, "A New System of the Nature and the Communication of Substances, As Well As the Union Between the Soul and the Body," in LL 2.739-752, at 741 (emphasis added).
14. PT, 117-118.

atoms or particles of matter cohere, nor for how they are regulated in complex organisms. This chain of logic leads Leibniz to a rather significant proposition: *"Extension"* and *"property,"* since they both lack sentience, will, or any means whatsoever of carrying out intentions, *cannot move matter,* that is, *they are not the source of their own movement.* Other of Leibniz's writings arrive at the same conclusion about extension as material essence, and are summed up nicely by Catherine Wilson: "A body is logically capable of assuming any shape and magnitude, [Leibniz] observes; hence the fact that it has the shape and size it does must be sought outside itself...".[15]

> Building upon his critique of atomism and Cartesian matter theory, Leibniz further proposes that body is neither substance nor essence because a substance, by definition, contains its own principle of action: "Since body is nothing other than matter and figure, and the cause of motion certainly cannot be understood either from matter or from figure, the cause of motion must be outside body."[16]

---

15. Catherine Wilson, "Leibniz and Atomism," *Studies in History and Philosophy of Science* 15 (1982), 175-199, at 181. On Leibniz and atomism, see also Richard T.W. Arthus, "The Enigma of Leibniz's Atomism," *Oxford Studies in Early Modern Philosophy* 1 (2003), 183-227; R. Bregmann, "Leibniz and Atomism," *Nature and System* 6 (1984), 237-248; and Milic Capek, "Leibniz's Thought Prior to the Year 1670: From Atomism to a Geometrical Kinetism," *Revue Internationale de Philosophie* 76-77 (1966), 249-256.
16. DA, 2.1.11. Cited in Maria Rosa Antognazza, *Leibniz: An Intellectual Biography* (Cambridge: Cambridge University Press, 2009), 104. Space considerations have precluded a more in-depth look at Leibniz's critique of the mechanical philosophy, but suffice to say that we have compressed this multivocal issue into a few linear arguments which, it is hoped, do minimal violence to the overall complexity of Leibniz's thought.

"Case In Point": A Platonic/Euclidean Metaphor in Leibniz's Philosophy of Science

Before we draw any further conclusions about his idiosyncratic approach to science, let us first explore Leibniz's most well known concept, that of the "formal atom," or "monad," all the while casting a backward glance at our foregoing discussion of Leibniz's critical response to Cartesianism in particular and to atom theory in general.

At the same time that he was virulently rejecting atomistic matter theory, Leibniz was becoming more and more enamored with Thomas Hobbes' *On Bodies*, and he shared with the great English philosopher a common postulate about the Euclidean point: The point has no parts, or at least its parts are so small as to have no assignable magnitude.[17] However, Leibniz goes farther than Hobbes in asserting that the extension or parts of a point are not only too small to be assigned a mathematical status, but are actually *unextended*: "A point is not that which has no parts... but rather whose extension is nil."[18]

The notion of a non-extended point is Leibniz's link between the realms of matter and soul, analogous to the "astral body" in Renaissance Platonism.[19] Leibniz thought that the non-extended point would allow science to actually explain more about motion and about bodies by acknowledging the metaphysical basis of all created essences. Of course, in an academic climate ruled by scientistic fundamentalism, the ascription of ultimate meaning to a non-material cause is often seen as a slamming of the door on science in favor of religion. Today, however, some modern physicists have followed Leibniz in refusing to give matter its own category of existence, instead viewing matter as a particular aspect or mode

---

17. See Thomas Hobbes, *The English Works of Thomas Hobbes of Malmesbury*, ed. Sir William Molesworth, 11 vols. (London, 1839-1845), 1.206.

18. DA, 265. Cited in Howard Bernstein, "Conatus, Hobbes, and the Young Leibniz," *Studies in History and Philosophy of Science* 11 (1980), 25-37, at 27.

19. On the Neoplatonic "astral body" in the context of the Renaissance, see D.P. Walker, "The Astral Body in Renaissance Medicine," *Journal of the Warburg and Courtauld Institutes* 21.1/2 (Jan.-Jun. 1958), 119-133.

of energy. At any rate, Leibniz's religio-philosophical copula was the non-extended point, which stood in his mind as the only possible bridge between science and theology, physics and metaphysics.

In order to see the implications of Leibniz's non-extended point for the rest of his thought, we will next touch on the scholastic distinction between matter and form, which Leibniz insisted was not to be thrown out. He considered forms to be "mind-monads," sentient emanations from the Divine Mind. It is difficult to explain Leibniz's notion of form in terms of "scientific revolution" or "new science," because his utilization of Neoplatonic concepts and strategies to connect the physical processes and realities of the material world to the spirit world is actually a variant on a long-established Scholastic practice.[20] Thus, Leibnitz's metaphysics is both revolutionary *and* conservative: Mechanical explanations must be used when describing the "*how*" of the material world and its processes, but the "*why*" or the "*ultimate how*" of every created being is simultaneously referred to the realm of spirit, of mind, which is perfectly ordered according to the unity of the Divine Mind.[21]

---

20. On Leibniz's Aristotelian physics and its inclusiveness, see Daniel Garber, "Leibniz: Physics and Philosophy," in *The Cambridge Companion to Leibniz*, ed. Nicholas Jolley (Cambridge: Cambridge University Press, 1995), 270-352. The following passage is particularly germane to our argument: "...Leibniz held that the essence of body is extension and impenetrability, as many mechanists did. However, unlike run-of-the-mill mechanists, Leibniz combined this view with an Aristotelian view of substance, holding that only constitute substances when taken together with concurrent minds, in particular, the mind of God, who is the source of activity in the world" (273).

21. "Thanks to the 'admirable' progress of science recorded in his own century, [Leibniz] argued, it had 'become apparent that mechanical explanations—reasons from the figure and motion of bodies, as it were—can be given for most of the things which the ancients referred only to the Creator or to some kind...of incorporeal forms.' (-) The key to avoiding the apparent atheistic consequences of modern science was to be found in the distinction between mechanical and metaphysical explanations of the universe, the latter of which began where 'mechanism' left off and then dug deeper to arrive at 'foundations and principles.' Rather than rejecting mechanical explanations of phenomena altogether..., Leibniz proposed merely to reject the premature claim that bodies were self-sufficient and could exist without an incorporeal principle" (Antognazza, *Leibniz*, 102, interior citation from DA 6.1.490).

Leibniz believes that at the heart of every existing body is a point *sans* extension, a non-material atom. Leibniz himself readily admits that his non-extended points—which he later calls "monads"—are a reintroduction of Aristotle's substantial form into physics![22] What Leibniz then does is quite bold, and, as we hinted above, should sound strangely familiar to our modern ears: He introduces a category called *vis viva*—energy—that is absent from Cartesianism. *Vis viva* constitutes both the soul-essence of monads as well as their activities and final goals. Matter, for Leibniz, far from having an essence, is only a lower type of energy. Specifically, matter is nothing more than the passive power of beings to slow things down (in fact, bodies for Leibniz are not essences but "accidents"[23]). Above this passive power of matter is the active power or energy of God that is the basis of monads and which constitutes their ability to freely actualize God's "pre-established harmony."[24]

Several points should here be noted about Leibniz's monadic energy, as well as its relation both to Leibniz's overall work and to the history of natural philosophy and theology. This list aims at more than mere summary, as it incorporates teachings of Leibniz and elements of his scholastic background not developed above:

> a.   *Vis viva* is functionally similar to the medieval Roman Catholic doctrine of God's supernatural grace/activity. A corollary to this "supernatural grace" teaching is the dogma of ideas in the mind of God that, according to Roman Catholic belief, exist in the Divine Essence as attributes of all created beings.[25] Leibnizian *vis viva* and supernatural

---

22. *G.W. Leibniz: Discourse On Metaphysics and Related Writings*, ed. R.N.D. Martin and Stuart Brown (Manchester and New York: Manchester University Press, 1988), 49-50.

23. DA, 6.1.509.

24. Brown and Fox, *Dictionary* 99-100. Also see G. Macdonald Ross, *Leibniz* (Oxford: Oxford University Press, 1984), 43-44.

25. Christia Mercer, *Leibniz's Metaphysics: Its Origins and Development* (Cambridge: Cambridge University Press, 2001), 209-11. Mercer shows the Neoplatonic basis of Leibniz's cosmology, as does Loemaker, "Herborn," 280-288, esp. 288, where Loemaker traces Leibniz's notion of ascent into forms in the essence of God back to its origin in Augustine. From Augustine, Loemaker attests, the

grace share a similar type of duality: 1) In relation
to creation, the grace of God/vis viva actualizes the
ideas/forms in the essence of God and which draw
all things to God in the form of "created graces."[26]
2) In relation to God's own essence or mind, grace/
vis viva can be seen as the movement or activity of
the Persons of the Trinity toward the all-good and
completely self-sufficient Divine Essence. Though
some of the specifics of this summary of scholastic grace theory may not be spelled out in his writings, Leibniz everywhere, in our view, uses the rich
tradition of scholasticism to show how all monads
move themselves because they are essentially ideas
in God's mind and are granted "force" or "grace" by
God to move harmoniously and freely toward their
beatific ends.

b.   Thus, through his monadic philosophy
Leibniz has preserved the freedom of both God and
creation, and he has preserved the distinction between creation and God. Further, he has explained
how matter constitutes a real unity through its ori-

---

notion of a Christian God full of accessible ideas is carried through the Francis-
cans, Nicholas Cusanus, and the Renaissance Neoplatonists to Leibniz via the
Herborn encyclopedists.
26. Leibniz in countless places expounds his variant on the Augustinian/scho-
lastic mysticism of man's mind as a reflection of ideas in the essence of God.
The following quotation shows Leibniz's Roman Catholic "Idea mysticism," which
the great German polymath discusses in the context of Malebranche's notion,
irresistible to the Hermetically inclined Leibniz, that humans think all of their
thoughts through God's ideas! "As to whether we see all things in God...or
whether all ideas are our own, we must realize that even if we do see all things
in God, it is still necessary for the ideas through which we see to be our own at
the same time; that is, our ideas are not little replicas, so to speak, but affections
or modifications corresponding to what we perceive in God" (Wiener, Selections, 289-290). In *On the Ultimate Origin of Things*, Leibniz speaks of the ideas
of all created beings as existing inside the essence of God: "They [the essences
of things or the possibles] exist in a certain region of ideas, if I may thus speak,
that is in God himself" (Cited in William E. May, "The God of Leibniz," *New Scholasticism* 36 (1962), 506-528, at 519, note 50). On Leibniz's hermetic proclivities
see the number of insightful essays in Allison Coudert, Richard Henry Popkin,
and Gordon M. Weiner (eds.), *Leibniz, Mysticism, and Religion* (Dordrecht: Kluwer
Academic Publishers, 1998).

gin and grounding in the realm of immaterial souls and in the highest Soul, the Trinitarian God.

c.   Leibniz sees matter as a secondary reflection of the soul-world of monads, the soul-world of monads being a collection of thought-forms in the mind of God. God is the *One*, this One being both the first religious *and* the first philosophical principle of St. Augustine, and as such the One is the Monad of monads and the apex of the great chain of being. The basis of Leibniz's great chain of harmonious monads is the Neoplatonic Christianity of St. Augustine of Hippo and his followers in the Middle Ages and even today.[27]

This section has tried to show the place of natural philosophy in Leibniz to be at once central and peripheral, for though natural science can bring us "happiness," it is only because man as a sentient monad sees the Monad (God) reflected there, and can ascend to the source of rational truth by developing his power of *perception*, which is tantamount to *reason*.[28] The material world reflects the One, and it has no essence of its own. However, it is the best of all possible worlds, and it is a true reflection of the unity of God, this unity being the primary attribute of divinity. As for Leibniz's relation to the new science of his day, Vennebusch offers a summation: "Leibniz combines acceptance of a consistent mechanism with a decisive rejection of an absolute mechanism. He accepts the thesis that all physical processes can be explained mechanically; but he also sees that one can, nevertheless, retain the teleological view handed down to us from antiquity...".[29]

27. Leibniz's own words can be used to show that his Neoplatonic sympathy was deeply felt since his childhood: "As a boy I studied Aristotle, and even the Scholastics were not repulsive to my tastes.... But at that time Plato, and with him Plotinus, gave me especial joy" (*Lettre a Mortmort*, in *God. Guil. Leibnitii opera philosophica quae extant latine, gallica, germainica omnia*, ed. J.E. Erdmann [Berlin, 1840], 701-702. Cited in J. Politella, *Platonism, Aristotelianism, and Cabalism in the Philosophy of Leibniz* [Philadelphia: University of Pennsylvania, 1938], 11).
28. LL 1.431-447.
29. Joachim Vennebusch, *Gottfried Wilhelm Leibniz: Philosopher and Politician in the Service of a Universal Culture* (Bad Godesberg, Germany: Inter Nationes,

As we move into our next section, which deals with Leibniz's ecumenism, it should be kept in mind that the great monadologist's mechanical teleology, his scientific metaphysics, is based on a kind of Neoplatonic rationalism. The *telos* of humanity is a rational ascent to God, who is the only infinitely rational being, and thus the only being totally free of materiality.[30] Religious strife is the result of nonconformity to the perfect rationality of God. The same scientific rationality which allows us to predict the movements of bodies in space and time also exists as the ladder that leads to perfect *eudaemonia*, to complete satisfaction of all spiritual desires in God.

1966), 32

30. *Monadology* § 72.

Chapter Ten

Leibniz's Irenicism

Leibniz and Ecumenism

G.J. Jordan calls Gottfried Wilhelm Leibniz "the greatest supporter of Church unity that the world has yet known."[31] In her erudite intellectual biography of the great philosopher, Maria Rosa Antognazza speaks of Leibniz's ecumenism as the core of the overarching goal which spanned his whole life, the creation of "an all-embracing encyclopaedic plan of reform and advancement of the sciences for the promotion of the common good...."[32] In fact, as we hinted in the previous section, Leibniz's encyclopedic project proposed to establish sciences such as mathematics, geometry, and physics on a sure footing by writing a completely clear and accurate set of rules and applications for accepting reasoned propositions. Once the proper rules were accepted, then controversies would subside. Leibniz's second step is crucial, and gives us some idea of the intention and inspiration of his scientific ecumenism: The physical "sciences were not to be pursued as ends in themselves but as preconditions for the demonstration of the existence of God and the defense of the Christian mysteries. From the new philosophy of mind... which he was

---

31. G.J. Jordan, *The Reunion of the Churches: A Study of G.W. Leibniz and His Great Attempt* (London: Constable and Co. Ltd., 1927), 31.

32. Antognazza, *Leibniz*, 233. For full bibliographies on Leibniz's ecumenism, see Kurt Müller, *Leibniz-Bibliographie: die Literatur über Leibniz bis 1980* (Frankfurt am Main: Vittorio Klostermann, 1984), 83-89; and Kurt Müller, *Leibniz-Bibliographie, Band 2. Die Literatur über Leibniz, 1981-1990* (Frankfurt am Main: Vittorio Klostermann, 1996), 21.

developing, Leibniz explained to Arnauld, he dared to promise 'some considerable light' on the defense of the controversial mysteries of the Trinity, the Incarnation, predestination, and the Eucharist."[33] The rules of reason properly established would end political, philosophical and religious controversies. Our consideration of Leibniz's ecumenism will be bipartite. The first section will analyze the "*Regulae circa Christianorum omnium ecclesiasticam unionem*," a Leibnizian document that outlines procedural rules for church union. The *Regulae* was the result of an irenicist conference in which Leibniz played an integral role. In the second part, we will look at some secondary literature dealing with Leibniz's plans for church reunion, paying extra attention to a significant but heretofore unnoticed piece by Jean Guitton which makes many startling assertions concerning Leibniz's ecumenical scheme.

The Interfaith Conference at Hanover (1683)

During Leibniz's tenure as librarian of the ducal library, the Duke of Hanover Ernest Augustus summoned Lutheran irenics, including Gerhard Wolter Molanus and Friedrich Ulrich Calixt, to a conference with the Roman Catholic ecumenist Christopher Rojas de Spinola, Titular Bishop of Tina (Croatia) and afterwards (1686) Bishop of Neustadt.[34] The gathering took place at the Hanoverian royal residence, and the document that resulted from it—"*Regulae circa Christianorum omnium ecclesiasticam unionem*"—was composed with the cooperation of Leibniz, who was then acting as an unofficial advisor to the group. After the drafting of the *Regulae*, Leibniz often expressed his full approval of the document in various epistolary and literary contexts.[35]

---

33. Ibid., 92. Antognazza's citation of Leibniz's letter to Arnauld is found in DA 2.1.173.
34. Jordan, *Reunion*, 53.
35. Marcelo Dascal, "Introductory Essay," in *Gottfried Wilhelm Leibniz: The Art of Controversies*, ed. and trans. Marcelo Dascal with Quintín Racionero and Adelino Cardoso (Dordrecht, The Netherlands: Springer, 2008), ix-lxxii. Not only at Hanover

The *Regulae* proposed that both parties—Lutheran and Roman Catholic—should engineer a reunion of the churches by declaring themselves already united *simply by virtue of their mutual acknowledgment of the union.* Both groups were to move forward as "Old Catholics" and "New Catholics," the latter being former Lutherans and the "Old Catholics" being former Roman Catholics. Occasional intercommunion would then be offered in select parishes where the clergy and laity were already sympathetic to the irenicist cause, these Lutherans and Catholics then pressing on under the assumption that the Council of Trent was suspended until a new ecumenical council could be called.[36] Note the diplomatic genius of Leibniz and his collaborators' three-part scheme, which may be listed as "1) assumption of unity, 2) intercommunion, and 3) appeal to council." First of all, the scheme proposes that a small group of educated elites (a group already sympathetic to irenicism) hidden away from the turbulence of the public sphere proclaim a *de facto* union, even going so far as to call both groups "Catholic," though distinguished by the labels "Old" and "New." Ironically, this self-proclaimed authority, once given broader currency through scattered liturgical affirmation, proposes to call an ecumenical council to straighten out the divisive and unacceptable aspects of the Council of Trent, since the latter council lacks ecumenicity.

This plan allows the Lutherans, along with all other Reformist Protestants on the sidelines, to have the bottom-up reforms of the Church for which Luther and other "reasonable men" have clamored, since the initiative comes, not from Rome, but from Luther's home base. On the other hand, the Roman Catholics are appeased because, in the final analysis, authority resides within the principle of conciliarity, and nowhere does the *Regulae* indicate that a true ecumenical council is anything

---

in 1683, but also in many of the religious negotiations in which he was involved, Leibniz "remained at the backstage, letting the official initiatives [such as Spinola] play the leading role. In particular, he took care of the methodological, historical, and doctrinal aspects of the debates. He was, however, an important figure in such negotiations and spent an enormous amount of work in them" (xxix).

36. Jordan, *Reunion*, 53-55.

but the Pope and all the bishops gathered together to proclaim the mind of the Church.

Other strategies are evinced in the text of the *Regulae*, which consists in a number of procedural rules for proper irenicist pursuits. Rule 1: "…[E]very Christian is bound to give his help as far as lies within his power and in accordance with the laws of God and man of those of the Diets of the Empire. Those who proclaim the opposite must be treated as heretics and as traitors."[37] Here the tactic is to redefine heresy as meaning "any opposition to the conference's specific ecumenical program." After all, the logic goes, opposing the reunion of Christendom is indefensible. Why would not any Christian wish to aid the effort at reunion? So, the Hanover group has subtly established itself as the arbiter of the Church's true boundary, and, in the group's hands, this boundary separates whoever agrees with the Hanover program from everyone else in the world.

Another of the *Regulae's* strategies is to cite a particular Protestant sect's practices which are similar to those of Roman Catholics in order to plea for tolerance of Roman practices as non-essential pieties. For example, those of the reformed Helvetic Confession "fall on their knees before the Eucharistic Bread and receive it in this posture."[38] The Hanover document's logic on this point may be extrapolated thusly: As Protestants, we are currently tolerant of the Helvetians, and we have never once thought about denying that they are part of the Church. Roman Catholics, however, we often deem heretics because they venerate the Host. This unequal treatment, by definition, is prejudicial. To be consistent, we must tolerate the liturgical and eucharistic idiosyncrasies of the Roman Catholics in the same way that we tolerate those of the Helvetic Confession.

A third trend is also found in the *Regulae*—we can name it dogmatic utilitarianism. According to this principle certain changes to tradition are foregone (at least as a stage preliminary to their introduction) due to the prejudice of the people.[39]

---

37. Ibid., 56.
38. Ibid.
39. Txetxu Ausín explicitly links Leibniz's irenicism with an "[e]thical consequen-

Though a practice may be correct and even necessary, its use must be dictated by what will be accepted by a group of worshippers, and any pious practice or teaching must be weighed against its purported reception by the laity: "...Catholics will not endure an immediate abolition of their forms of prayer, liturgy and ceremonies; nor will they be obliged to receive the Sacrament from the hands of a priest whom they deem to be of doubtful Orders."[40]

Here we will draw a tentative conclusion about Leibniz's scientific rationalism and its application in his ecumenist efforts, though it must be stressed that this is intended as nothing more than a possible direction for further research. Just as Leibniz seems to favor a Neoplatonic valuation of a spiritual/noetic world over an "accidental" material world, so he has no problem justifying the alteration of external ritual practices to serve the greater goal of spiritual, inner Church unity.[41] Leibniz in many places assumes a dichotomy between an Inner and an outer Church, and it is obvious that he, to some degree, aligns this Inner/outer Church binary with his Platonic

tialism, close to some utilitarian approaches...." ("Weighing and Gradualism in Leibniz as Instruments for the Analysis of Normative Conflicts," *Studia Leibnitiana* 37.1 (2005), 99-111, at 106; see also idem, "The Quest for Rationalism Without Dogmas in Lebniz and Toulmin," in D. Hitchcock and B. Verheff (eds.), *Arguing on the Toulmin Model: New Essays in Argument Analysis and Evaluation* [Dordrecht: Springer, 2006], 261-272, at 266).

40. Jordan, *Reunion*, 59-60.

41. A similar conclusion about Leibniz's devaluation of ritual and other "externals" of the Christian faith is reached by Steven Nadler in his *The Best of All Possible Worlds: A Story of Philosophers, God, and Evil* (New York: Farrar, Straus and Giroux, 2008): "Much of the problem, [Leibniz] insisted, lay not in basic dogma but in the particular, nonessential beliefs and customs that had developed within each tradition. 'Most of the objections that can be made against Rome regard the practice of the people rather than the dogmas,' he wrote in 1682. If only one could discover and properly interpret the core beliefs that unite all Christians—and distill them from the layers of ecclesiastic organization, ceremonial observance, and sectarian understanding within which they had become encrusted—there would be a possibility of reuniting the faithful within a single church" (10). It cannot be doubted that Leibniz's "spiritualist" tendency in theology comes from his Hermetico-Platonic view of matter as "of the same kind as the monad or else... a nothing, a privation, a ghostly limit," as R.E. Butts holds in his insightful piece "Leibniz' Monads: A Heritage of Gnosticism and a Source of Rational Science," *Canadian Journal of Philosophy* 10.1 (March 1980): 47-62, at 52.

mind/matter opposition, the latter term in both formulations being subordinated to the more rational, and thus more real, "mind" realm.[42] However, it must be noted that the latter term, the "outer/ritual/material" half, the part which corresponds to natural science, is not completely devalued, especially as it points, through its reflected harmony, all monads to the ultimate monad, God.

Jean Guitton on Leibniz's Ecumenism: The Ecumeno-scientific Superorder

Jean Guitton's "Leibniz and Pascal: Protestantism, Catholicism and Ecumenicism"[43] seeks to understand Leibniz's ecumenism in the context of his attitudes toward the science of his day (17th century). In this wise, Guitton's focus could not be more germane to our purpose, since his essay analyzes the connection between the two aspects of Leibniz's thought—ecumenism and science—that have been the subjects of the preceding two chapters of this section.

First of all, Guitton establishes Leibniz's lifelong fascination with and idealization of the Roman Catholic Society of Jesus, known as the Jesuit Order. Specifically, Guitton notes that Leibniz believed the Jesuit order to be, at least in its inner inspiration and purpose, the key to Church unity—and along with it, the unity of society as a whole—in a scientific age that was growing more and more suspicious of both a heavy-handed Roman Church and an equally directionless Protestantism:

---

42. See the following, from a letter written by Leibniz to the Landgrave Ernest dated January 1684: "I believe that a person may be a member of the Invisible Communion of the Church Catholic without being in the Visible Church; as when a person is unjustly excommunicated by an error or by the malice of the Judge" (ibid., 39).

43. Jean Guitton, "Leibniz and Pascal: Protestantism, Catholicism and Ecumenicism," *Cross Currents* 4.1 (Fall 1953), 12-35. Orig. published as ch. 9-10 in Jean Guitton, *Pascal et Leibniz: étude deux types de penseurs* (Paris: Aubier, 1951), 123-152 (in French).

The Jesuit institution, far from representing in his eyes the most perfidious opposition to the true Christian spirit and the mentality of the Early Church, is the most remarkable development of this primitive Christianity. The faults of the Society, as serious as they are, are extrinsic. Intrinsically the order is sound. And, if this order had been reformed along the lines of its essential character, it could have procured for the Apostolate means of an expansion which meet modern requirements in its double mission, interior and exterior.[44]

Guitton points out Leibniz's desire to see the formation of a Jesuit-styled super-order, a "more comprehensive Order" which would incorporate all of the best elements of each of the existing Catholic orders into a single group. It is obvious that Leibniz saw the best elements of Christianity as 1) its compatibility with reason and science and 2) its hierarchical organization, with bishops, orders and Pope at the apex of the structure. Here we will supply a lengthy quotation to give the reader a feel for Guitton's presentation of Leibniz's thinking on this most important of subjects:

> Leibniz had carefully analyzed the concept of *religious order*. He had worked out the conditions of the perfect adaptation of these orders to their end which, in his eyes, was the most efficacious realization of the Divine Plan. Leibniz's plan was to keep what was best in each existing order, then to incorporate these best elements into a more comprehensive Order. At the same time, each of the existing orders (at least those which were long established) was to profit by the current spirit which was a spirit of reason and science. Leibniz dreamed of

44. Ibid., 17. Donald F. Lach's "Leibniz and China" (*Journal of the History of Ideas* 6.4 [October 1945], 436-455) gives us a clue as to the reason for Leibniz's fixation on the Jesuit order. He apparently saw in the Jesuits' ecumenist strategy toward China a template for all Christian missionary endeavors. The Jesuits did not ask the Chinese to abandon their cultural traditions, specifically their Confucian social organization. Leibniz went a step further, considering the Confucian cultural achievement to be the greatest development of natural theology, while European Christianity was the height of revealed theology (441).

a Church where the Cistercians would be also natural-
ists, where the mendicant orders were also physicians,
the contemplatives also mathematicians, the learned orders also historians, the missionaries also linguists, the
theologians also critics, the liturgists also lovers of nature and its cycles. Leibniz feared that, with religious, all
powers of observation were confined to their liturgical
and pastoral duties in the narrow grooves understood as
proper to those offices before the dawn of the scientific
age. Leibniz hoped that the findings of science "would
be no less understood than others in apostolic activities."
"It is not required," he wrote to Père Jergus, "that they
spend their whole time in the confessional or thinking
out sermons and cases of conscience." Leibniz would ad-
vise a division of labor, one contingent setting out on the
Propagation of faith by missions, the other on the Justifi-
cation of faith through science. He was even scheming, it
was said, to combine the orders into one Supreme Order,
a super-Order, the order of Charity: Instituatur Societas
sive ordo caritatis, composi tus ex contemplativis et ac-
tivis; and from this order the pope would be chosen.[45]

If we follow Leibniz's logic as presented by Guitton, it becomes
difficult to avoid the following conclusion: Leibniz wanted to
see a seamless integration of science with a superorder-led
Christianity. Perhaps Leibniz believed that, once the completely rational superorder was in place, then the whole wide world
of reasonable, scientific culture (including the Protestants)
would have no problem accepting a pope who was *primes inter
pares* in a society aligned totally with the same rational principles to which everyone already adhered.[46] Guitton expounds

---

45. Guitton, 17-18.
46. Guitton emphasizes that Leibniz was prescient in seeing that if the Church
did not adapt itself to the then-new scientific paradigm, then modern man
would leave the Church behind. On this theme, he quotes one of Leibniz's letters to Antoine Arnauld: "Today's most crying need is a very profound knowledge of religion. Why? Because a philosophical age is opening where, in the
natural and logical course of events, insistence on absolute accuracy in detail is
going to spread from the classrooms out into every walk of life. If we cannot sat-
isfy this demand for exact knowledge, the genuine propagation of religion must
be abandoned. Very soon the majority of men will be Christian only in externals;

the further theological implications of Leibniz's scientific ecumenism: "[For Leibniz], the application of reason to nature was going to replace the older theology which had been, for the most part, an application of reason to grace."[47]

This chapter has sought to explore some of the implications of Leibniz's scientific ecumenism, placing it in the context of the science of his day and also in the context of the Neoplatonic scholasticism that, for many scholars, is the basis for the *Monadology*. We have concluded that the "monad" notion is inspired by the "astral body" category of Renaisssance Neoplatonism and also by the Euclidean theory that was still central to many of Leibniz's contemporaries. Further, we have suggested that the same Neoplatonic metaphysic which led to Leibniz's monad also led to his valuation of imagined immaterial essentials and his devaluation of ritual and "externals" which did not correspond to Leibniz's idiosyncratic conception of a scientific super-order which would supply the only possible all-embracing socio-religious bond. Throughout our analysis it has been shown that Leibniz's science cannot be considered apart from his theology, specifically his rationalistic ecumenism.

---

enterprising persons with bad spirit will work for the destruction of the faith. Atheism with naturalism will be popular heresies" (ibid., 19).
47. Ibid., 18.

Lebniz's *Instrumentum Arithmeticum*, a 17th century forerunner of today's computers

Epilogue

Anatomyzing Divinity

We *live in a digital age.* Despite its banality this modern axiom nonetheless unlocks a great truth (*the* truth?) about modernity, a truth upon which this study strives to cast light.

What is the distinguishing mark of *digital* technology? It is based upon a fundamental opposition between "0" and "1." The former is "off," the latter "on." Leibniz, who was shocked to discover what he believed to be a proto-digital code in the *I-Ching's* broken and unbroken lines, viewed the digital dyad as a *process.* "Explication de l'arithmetique binaire," Leibniz's presentation of binary arithmetic appeared in 1703, and was "the first public presentation on this topic to result in a significant impact on the scientific community."[1] Boole and the great minds at Bell Labs—in the 19th and 20th centuries, respectively—connected the necessary dots, and the seemingly infinite practical applications of binary code began to become apparent. Nothing could be more "apparent" than *qualitatively new reality*, new machines that change, rearrange, and expand the horizons of human culture and thought.

Who, indeed, would gainsay that computers and the microprocessors that undergird modern machines have wrought such a sea-change in our lives? But are these amazing technological advances based only on Leibniz's mathematical insights, or do they also retain a link with the great German thinker's *metaphysics*? Would G.W. Leibniz have partitioned

---

1. Anton Glaser, *History of Binary and Other Nondecimal Numeration*, revised ed. (Tomash Publishers, 1981), 39. Avail. online at: http://www.eipiphiny.org/books/history-of-binary.pdf.

off his mathematics (with its applications in the world of engineering) from his theology? Let us consider Leibniz's plan for a "binary medallion," which he revealed in his letter of January 2, 1697 to Rudolph August, Duke of Brunswick. Though lengthy, our excerpt gives us the kind of detail we need to make the proper assessment of Leibniz's binary arithmetaphysics:

> And so that I won't come entirely empty-handed this time, I enclose a design of that which I had the pleasure of discussing with you recently. It is in the form of a memorial coin or medallion; and though the design is mediocre and can be improved in accordance with your judgment, the thing is such, that it would be worth showing in silver now and unto future generations, if it were struck at your Highness's command. Because one of the main points of the Christian Faith, and among those points that have penetrated least into the minds of the worldly-wise and that are difficult to make with the heathen is the creation of all things out of nothing through God's omnipotence, it might be said that nothing is a better analogy to, or even *demonstration of* such creation than the *origin of numbers* as here represented, using only unity and zero or nothing. And it would be difficult to find a better illustration of this secret in nature or philosophy; hence I have set on the medallion design *IMAGO CREATONIS* [in the image of creation].
>
> It is no less remarkable that there appears therefrom, not only that God made everything from nothing, but also that everything that He made was good; as we can see here, with out own eyes, in this image of creation. Because instead of there appearing no particular order or pattern, as in the common representation of numbers, there appears here in contrast a wonderful order and harmony which cannot be improved upon. Inasmuch as the rule of alternation provides for continuation, so that one can write without computation or the aid of memory as far as one wishes, if one alternates the last place 0,1,0,1,0,1, etc., putting these under each other; and then putting under each other in the second place (from the right) 0,0,1,1,0,0,1,1, etc.; in the third 0,0,0,0; 1,1,1,1; 0,0,0,0; 1,1,1,1; etc; in the fourth

0,0,0,0,0,0,0,0; 1,1,1,1,1,1,1,1; 0,0,0,0,0,0,0,0; 1,1,1,1,1,1,1,1; and so forth, the period or cycle of change becomes again as large for each new place. Such harmonious order and beauty can be seen in the small table on the medallion up to 16 or 17; since for a larger table, say to 32, there is not enough room. One can further see that the disorder, which one imagines in the work of God, is but apparent; that if one looks at the matter with the proper perspective, there appears symmetry, which encourages one more and more to love and praise the wisdom, goodness, and beauty of the highest good, from which all goodness and beauty has flown. I am corresponding with Jesuit Father Grimaldi, who is currently in China and also president of the Mathematics Tribunal there, with whom I became acquainted in Rome, and who wrote me during his return trip to China from Goa. I have found it appropriate to communicate to him these number representations in the hope, since he had told me himself that the monarch of this mighty empire was a lover of the art of arithmetic and that he had learned to figure the European way from Father Verbiest, Grimaldi's predecessor, that it might be this *image of the secret of creation* which might serve to show him more and more the excellence of the Christian faith. So that I may explain the rest of the medallion I marked the main places, namely 10 or 2, 100 or 4, 1000 or 8, 10000 or 16, with * or an asterisk, because if one takes note of these, one is bound to see the origin of the remaining numbers. For example, why 1101 stands before 13 is shown by this demonstration:

1	1
00	0
100	4
1000	8
1101	13

and so it is with all other numbers. I have also given an example of addition and one of multiplication on the medallion at the sides of the table so that one could note from them the foundation of operations and how the arithmetic rules apply here too."[2]

---

2. Ibid., 31–35. Emphasis added.

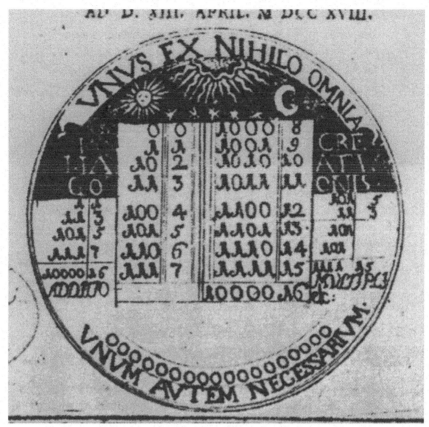

Leibniz's Design of the Binary Medallion, appearing in Wiedeburg's *Dissertatio Mathematica*.

In this amazing letter, Leibniz's concept of binary 0-1 arithmetic is presented as the only proper model for 1) the origin of numbers; 2) the creation of the cosmos by God; and 3) the nature of both this creative process and its qualities of "symmetry" and "goodness."

However, as Part 3 demonstrated, if we consider Leibniz's philosophical writings, we see many connections to the Platonized Christianity that, in its various permutations, has guided (even constituted) Western theology from Augustine of Hippo to the present. Thus, Leibniz definitely believes in an *analogia entis*, a true ontological analogy between creation and the Creator. In light of this, we can add a fourth context and a fifth context for the binary medallion's 0-1 model: 4) the pattern of the unfolding of all created beings; and 5) the pattern of the infolded being of the Persons of the Trinity. Moreover, Leibniz's sketch of the binary medallion links modern technology to our starting point: alchemy. The sky depicted in the sketch has the sun and moon in the left and right halves of the sky. In alchemical symbolism, this "sun and moon sky" indicates the deification of matter and man as the fruit of the Great Work.

Leibniz's mathematical theology might be epitomized as follows: *"Zero" is the radically simple, all-encompassing Monad, undeveloped and unscissioned. The "one" is the developed Monad, developed because differentiated. The Monad longs to long, to move toward Itself.*

But this is far from all. As we stated in our brief overview above, digital technology is based upon the 0-1 meta-opposition. But what is being opposed?

.... Bits! ....

So, what is a "bit"?

*** *** ***

I envisioned this, the book's concluding section, as an answer to the anticipated query, "why should anyone living in the here and now care about all of this?" Let us look no further than our own computers for a ready answer. Specifically, observe the pixels on your computer screen (and notice, I need not ask *if* you have a computer, just as, forty years ago, one might have written "look outside at *your* automobile..."). We look at photographs and films that seem to be real, that is, we think we are looking through a window or some foot-wide peephole in the same manner that we take in the world with our eyes. However, our computer screens present to our eyes nothing more than a grid of tiny square cells.

Each cell is a solid color. I cannot speak for you, dear reader, but I feel this fact to be highly counterintuitive. I see depth, contour, and...reality (for lack of a better word) when I view *Juliet of the Spirits* or a baseball game on my PC's monitor.

So, a few words about these monochrome squares: Each cell's color can be either one of the three primary ones, or it can be white, or it can be black, or it can be some mixture of primaries and/or white/black. Without going into technical details, let us note that an 8-bit pixel has 255 different possible shades. These 255 possibilities are different states between 0 (color completely off, or black) and 255 (color completely on). Look at this discontinuous digital continuum as a string of 255 different combinations of "ons" and "offs" on a switch box that has 8 switches on it. For 24-bit pixel technology, as found in the latest digital cameras and such, there are 3 such switch boxes (with a total of 24 switches), one for each primary color. The point is that the most complex, lifelike simulacra imaginable (home movies or digital photos taken of family and friends, for instance), when you dig deep enough, find their origin in a large set of 0-1 choices. The following definition of "digital," taken from the Internet, puts us on the trail of further insights:

> Describes any system based on discontinuous data or events. Computers are digital machines because at their most basic level they can distinguish between just two values, 0 and 1, or off and on. There is no simple way to represent all the values in between, such as 0.25. All data that a computer processes must be encoded digitally, as a series of zeroes and ones.
>
> The opposite of digital is *analog*. A typical analog device is a clock in which the hands move continuously around the face. Such a clock is capable of indicating every possible time of day. In contrast, a digital clock is capable of representing only a finite number of times (every tenth of a second, for example).
>
> In general, humans experience the world analogically. Vision, for example, is an analog experience because we perceive infinitely smooth gradations of shapes and colors. Most analog events, however, can be simulated digitally. Photographs in newspapers, for instance, consist of an array of dots that are either black or white. From afar, the viewer does not see the dots (the digital form), but

only lines and shading, which appear to be continuous. Although digital representations are approximations of analog events, they are useful because they are relatively easy to store and manipulate electronically. The trick is in converting from analog to digital, and back again.[3]

It is interesting to note—in light of this passage and the Leibniz letter—that physicalists and reductionists who write polemical attacks on religion would seem to agree with Leibniz that complex processes in nature are "reducible" rather than "emergent" in that they do not represent anything qualitatively new, but rather seem so from the limited nature of our senses and mental processes (and Leibniz, as we will see, thinks that all of the possibilities of each atom's nature are enfolded inside it!). For instance, as John R. Searle once explained in an interview, we sense water flowing through our hands as wet, but "wet" is not a property of individual atoms of H2O, but rather refers to how a mass of water feels as millions of atoms of it course over our skin.

In a sense, emergent properties do not "exist" outside of the minds/senses of those who experience them. This same notion is employed by Searle and others who believe that consciousness and all "higher level" reality is a kind of trick that our bodies play on us by giving us a strong sense that there are qualitatively different levels of reality, when in actuality there are only atoms and the void.

Technology seems to constitute support for the "non-emergence" model, since a computer's mind-bogglingly complex operations can be reduced to the 0-1 metabinary. When the argument for reductionism is posed with this technological metaphor, we are left with either accepting reductionism or positing a "ghost in the machine," or some equally arbitrary supernatural emergence. I mean, honestly, could anyone actually believe that computer assembly lines are, in any sense of the word, soul factories?

However, Leibniz's notion of "monads," which in one sense agrees with the reductionists, upon further scrutiny turns

---

3. "digital." Avail. online at: http://www.webopedia.com/TERM/D/digital.html.

out to be a wrench in their gears. Let us paraphrase Leibniz's thoughts: Material reality is composed of monads—non-material "unities"—that are "windowless" in that they cannot be penetrated by any other monad or created being. These monads are immaterial, or at least the simplest material things imaginable.

If there are computers, societies, and ecosystems that exist, this is not *merely* because new properties emerge (or, as reductionists would have it, *seem* to emerge) from atoms, but also because God has placed *within* each monad all of the possibilities of its individual development. In fact, God has harmonized all of the possible developmental paths of all monads through his predeterminations, though He does not coerce but rather "inclines" each monad toward its *telos*. Thus, though no monad has "contact" with any other monad, every conscious being experiences the outside world and other beings as if they are interacting. In fact, Leibniz believes that humans *do* freely interact, but their monads, being immaterial, do not affect one another *internally*. The material world is not an illusion in Leibniz's scheme, but it definitely is not a direct window into the interiors of monads, though the natural world does *reflect* the "pre-established harmony" established and maintained by God.

*** *** ***

Let us conclude with the image of Gottfried Wilhelm Leibniz, giddy over his "binary medallion" proposal, his quill alternating between nimble bobs into the inkwell and blotless jots and tittles scratched onto a milk-white page of indestructible rag paper and ask ourselves a couple of questions:

1. Would Leibniz, without Pythagoras and his tetraktys, have concluded that a "1," a monas or monad at the tip of a cosmogonic pyramid, would serve as a model both for an interconnected cosmos and a transcendent deity?

2. Could the German polymath's intriguing design for the medallion retain its mystique without that alchemical sun-and-moon skyline, symbolizing the providential goal of God, man, and cosmos?

Fini

Illustrations

Figure 1: Illustration from Paraldus's *Summa of Vice* of a knight wielding the *Scutum fidei*. London BL Harl. 3244, fol. 28r. (pp. 14, 17, 21ff., 29, 33, 41). Citation from Evans, "Paraldus's Summa," pl. 3, following p. 68.

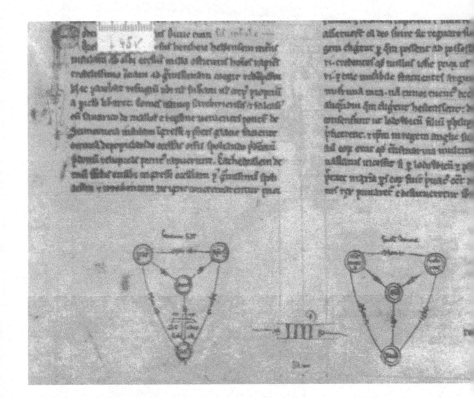

Figure 2: Matthew Paris, *Chronica majora*, fol. 45v, detail: the Augustinian analogy of the Holy Trinity and the parts of the soul. The shield of the trinity and the
shield of the soul. Citation from Evans, "Peraldus's Summa," pl. 4c, following p. 68.

Figure 3: Detail of Robert Hooke's Engraved Image of an Ink Jot Viewed Through a Microscope (*Micrographia*, plate following pg. 1). Notice the gold/sun symbol beside the "A."

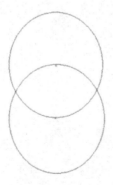

Figure 4. Author's rendering of the hermetic dual circle.

Figure 5. The alchemical sage "squaring the circle." (M. Meier, *Atalanta fugiens* [Oppenheim, 1618]).

Figure 6. From *Aurora consurgens*, early 16th century.

Figure 7. Otto II in Majesty (Stephan Beissel, *Die Bilder der Handschrift des Kaisers Otto im Münster zu Aachen* [Aachen, 1886], plate 3, after p. 61. Also in Kantorowicz, King's *Two Bodies*, fig. 5, plates following p. 512).

Figure 8. The great seal of Philip III and the great seal of Philip the Fair. Paris, Archives nationals D 45, 37 (Cited from Brown, "Persona et Gesta," 239).

Figure 9. The secret seal of Philip the Fair. Archives nationals d 48bis. (Cited in Favier, ff. p. 294)

Bibliography

Ahlstrom, Sydney E. *A Religious History of the American People.* 2nd ed. New Haven and London: Yale University Press, 2004 (1972).

Aghiorgoussis, M. [Met. Maximos of Pittsburgh] "Applications of the Theme 'EIKON THEOU' (Image of God) according to Saint Basil the Great." *Greek Orthodox Theological Review* 21.3 (Fall 1976): 265-288.

Albanese, Catherine L. *A Republic of Mind and Spirit: A Cultural History of American Metaphysical Religion.* New Haven and London: Yale University Press, 2007.

Ambrose, Elizabeth Ann. "*Cosmos, Anthropos,* and *Theos*: Dimensions of the Paracelsian Universe." *Cauda Pavonis* 11.1 (1992): 1-7.

Antognazza, Maria Rosa. *Leibniz: An Intellectual Biography.* Cambridge: Cambridge University Press, 2009.

Arthus, Richard T.W. "The Enigma of Leibniz's Atomism." *Oxford Studies in Early Modern Philosophy* 1 (2003): 183-227.

Ausín, Txetxu. "The Quest for Rationalism Without Dogmas in Lebniz and Toulmin." In *Arguing on the Toulmin Model: New Essays in Argument Analysis and Evaluation.* Ed. D. Hitchcock and B. Verheff. Dordrecht: Springer, 2006. 261-272.

---. "Weighing and Gradualism in Leibniz as Instruments for the Analysis of Normative Conflicts." *Studia Leibnitiana* 37.1 (2005): 99-111.

Baldwin, Martha. "Alchemy and the Society of Jesus in the Seventeenth Century: Strange Bedfellows." *Ambix* 40 (1993): 41-64.

Ball, Philip. "Alchemical Culture and Poetry in Early Modern England." *Interdisciplinary Science Reviews* 30.1 (2006): 77-92.

Bardi, Jason Socrates. *The Calculus Wars: Newton, Leibniz, and the Greatest Mathematical Clash of All Time.* New York: Thunder's Mouth Press, 2006.

Barnes, Jonathan. Review of Peter Kingsley, *Ancient Philosophy, Mystery and Magic. International Journal of the Classical Tradition* 4.3 (Winter, 1998): 460-462.

---. *Early Greek Philosophy.* 2nd revised edition. London: Penguin, 2001.

Barrett, William. *Irrational Man: A Study in Existential Philosophy.* New York: Anchor Books, 1990 (1958).

Baynes, N.H. "Eusebius and the Christian Empire." *Annuaire de l'institut de philology et d'histoire orientales* 2 (1933-1934): 13-18.

Benton, William. "Lutheran Churches." In *The New Encyclopaedia Britannica in Thirty Volumes.* 15th ed. 11.198.

Bernstein, Howard. "*Conatus,* Hobbes, and the Young Leibniz." *Studies in History and Philosophy of Science* 11 (1980): 25-37.

Bertelli, Sergio. *The King's Body: Sacred Rituals of Power in Medieval and Early Modern Europe.* Translated by R. Burr Litchfield. University Park, PA: Pennsylvania State University Press, 2001 (1990).

Berthelot, Marcelin. *Collection des anciens alchemists grecs*. 4 vols. Paris: Steinhel, 1887-8.

---. *Les origines de l'alchimie*. Paris: Georges Steinheil, 1885.

Bloch, Marc. *Les rois thaumaturges: etude sur le caractere surnaturel attribue a la puissance royale, particulirement en France el en Angleterre*. Paris and Stasbourg: Publications de la Faculte des lettres de l'Universite de Strasbourg, fasc. I9, 1924. English translation J. E. Anderson. *The Royal Touch: Sacred Monarchy and Scrofula in England and France*. London, 1973.

Blumenthal, U.-R. *The Investiture Controversy: Church and Monarchy from the Ninth to the Twelfth Century*. Philadelphia, 1988.

Boase, T.S.R. *Boniface VIII*. London: Constable and Co., 1933.

Bregmann, R. "Leibniz and Atomism." *Nature and System* 6 (1984): 237-248.

Gnosis and Hermeticism from Antiquity to Modern Times. Ed. R. van den Broek and Wouter J. Hanegraaff. Albany, NY: State University of New York Press, 1998. 1-20.

Brown, Elizabeth A.R. *The Monarchy of Capetian France and Royal Ceremonial*. Aldershot: Variorum, 1991.

---. "*Persona et Gesta*: The Image and Deeds of the Thirteenth-Century Capetians. The Case of Philip the Fair." *Viator* 19 (1988): 219-246.

---. "The Prince is Father of the King: The Character and Childhood of Philip the Fair of France." *Mediaeval Studies* 49 (1987): 282-334.

Brown, Stuart. "Leibniz's Formative Years (1646-76): An Overview." In *The Young Leibniz and His Philosophy (1646-76)*. Ed. Stuart Brown. Dordrecht, The Netherlands: Kluwer Academic Publishers, 1999. 1-18.

Brown, Stuart, and N.J. Fox. *Historical Dictionary of Leibniz's Philosophy*. Lanham, MD: The Scarecrow Press, Inc., 2006.

Browne, C.A. "Rhetorical and Religious Aspects of Greek Alchemy." *Ambix* 2.3 (December 1946): 129-137 and 3.1 (May 1948): 15-25.

Burckhardt, Titus. *Alchemy: Science of the Cosmos, Science of the Soul*. Trans. William Stoddart. Louisville, KY: Fons Vitae, 1997.

Burkert, Walter. *Lore and Science in Ancient Pythagoreanism*. Translated by Edwin L. Minar, Jr. Cambridge, MA: Harvard University Press, 1972.

Butts, R.E. "Leibniz' Monads: A Heritage of Gnosticism and a Source of Rational Science." *Canadian Journal of Philosophy* 10.1 (March 1980): 47-62.

Călian, George-Florin. "*Alkimia Operativa* and *Alkimia Speculativa*: Some Modern Controversies On the Historiography of Alchemy." *Annual of Medieval Studies at CEU* 16 (2010): 166-190.

Cantor, Norman F. *Medieval History: The Life and Death of a Civilization*. 2nd Ed. New York: Macmillan; London: Collier-Macmillan, 1969.

Capek, Milic. "Leibniz's Thought Prior to the Year 1670: From Atomism to a Geometrical Kinetism." *Revue Internationale de Philosophie* 76-77 (1966): 249-256.

Carlyle, R.W. and A.J. *A History of Mediaeval Political Theory in the West*. 6 vols. Edinburgh and London: William Blackwood and Sons Ltd., 1903-1936.

Chang, Ku-Ming (Kevin). "Toleration of Alchemists as a Political Question: Transmutation, Disputation, and Early Modern Scholarship on Alchemy." *Ambix* 54.3 (2007): 245-273.

Cohen, H. Floris. *The Scientific Revolution: A Historiographical Inquiry* (Chicago and London: University of Chicago Press, 1994).

Copenhaver, Brian P. "Did Science Have a Renaissance?" *Isis* 83.3 (1992): 387-407.

Copenhaver, Brian P., ed. *Hermetica: The Greek Corpus Hermeticum and the Latin Asclepius in a New English Translation with Notes and Introduction*. Cambridge: Cambridge University Press, 1992.

Coudert, Allison, Richard Henry Popkin, and Gordon M. Weiner, eds. *Leibniz, Mysticism, and Religion*. Dordrecht, The Netherlands: Kluwer Academic Publishers, 1998.

Chryssavgis, John. *Ascent To Heaven: The Theology of the Human Person According to Saint John of the Ladder*. Brookline, MA: Holy Cross Orthodox Press, 1989.

Dascal, Marcelo. "Introductory Essay." In *Gottfried Wilhelm Leibniz: The Art of Controversie*. Ed. and translated by Marcelo Dascal with Quintín Racionero and Adelino Cardoso. Dordrecht, The Netherlands: Springer, 2008. ix-lxxii.

Davis, Tenney L. "Neglected Evidence in the History of Phlogiston Together with Observations on the Doctrine of Forms and the History of Alchemy." *Annals of Medical History* 6 (1924): 280-287.

---. "Pictorial Representations of Alchemical Theory." *Isis* 28.1 (1938): 73-86.

---. "The Problem of the Origins of Alchemy." *The Scientific Monthly* 43.6 (1936): 551-558.

D'Avray, D.L. *Death and the Prince: Memorial Preaching before 1350*. Oxford: Clarendon Press, 1994.

Dawkins, Richard. *The God Delusion*. Boston and New York: Houghton Mifflin, 2006.

Debus, Allen G. "Changing Perspectives On the Scientific Revolution," *Isis* 89.1 (March 1998): 66-81.

Descartes, Rene. *The Philosophical Writings of Descartes*. 3 vols. Translated by J. Cottingham et al. Cambridge: Cambridge University Press, 1984-1991.

DeVun, Leah. *Prophecy, Alchemy, and the End of Time: John of Rupescissa in the Late Middle Ages*. New York: Columbia University Press, 2009.

Dubs, H.H. "The Beginnings of Alchemy." *Isis* 38 (1947): 62-86.

Dumezil, Georges. *Archaic Roman Religion*. 2 vols. Translated by P. Krapp (Chicago: University of Chicago Press, 1966).

Dupuy, Pierre. *Histoire du differend d'entre le pape Boniface VIII et Philippe le Bel...* (Paris, 1655).

Eliade, Mercea. "The Forge and the Crucible: A Postscript." *History of Religions* 8.1 (1968): 74-88.

Enfield, William. *The History of Philosophy from the Earliest Times to the Beginning of the Present Century: Drawn Up from Brucker's Historia Critica Philosophiae.* 2 vols. London: J.F. Dove, 1819.

Evans, Michael. "The Geometry of the Mind: Scientific Diagrams and Medieval Thought." *Architectural Association Quarterly* 12.4 (1980): 32-55.

---. "An Illustrated Fragment of Peraldus's Summa of Vice: Harleian MS 3244." *Journal of the Warburg and Courtauld Institutes* 45 (1982): 14-68.

Evans, R.J.W. Review of Pamela H. Smith. *The Business of Alchemy: Science and Culture in the Holy Roman Empire.* Princeton: Princeton University Press, 1994. *English Historical Review* 111.444 (Nov. 1996): 1286-1287

Every, George. *The Byzantine Patriarchate, 451-1204.* London: SPCK, 1962.

Faivre, Antoine. "Esotericism." In *The Encyclopedia of Religion.* 16 vols. Ed. Mircea Eliade. New York: Macmillan; London: Collier Macmillan, 1987. 5.156-163.

---. "Hermetism." In *The Encyclopedia of Religion.* 16 vols. Ed. Mircea Eliade. New York: Macmillan; London: Collier Macmillan, 1987. 6.295-296.

Farrell, Joseph P. *The Giza Death Star Destroyed.* Kempton, IL: Adventures Unlimited Press, 2005.

---. *God, History, and Dialectic: The Theological Foundations of the Two Europes and Their Cultural Consequences.* Tulsa, OK: Seven Councils Press, 1997.

---. "Outline: Students' Syllabus Version, *God, History, and Dialectic: Explorations of the Philosophical and Theological Foundations of the Two Europes.*" Unpublished course syllabus, 1996.

---. "Partial Listing of *Christologies* of Classical Heresies and Gnostics," Unpublished typescript in author's possession. 5 unnumbered pages.

---. "Patristics One: Origen and the Crisis of the First Hellenization of the Gospel: Notes and Outlines by Joseph P. Farrell, D.Phil. (Oxon.)." Unpublished typescript in author's possession, n.d., 21 unnumbered pgs.

---. *The Philosopher's Stone: Alchemy and the Secret Research for Exotic Matter.* Port Townsend, WA: Feral House, 2009.

---. "A Theological Introduction to the Mystagogy of Saint Photios." Saint Photius. *The Mystagogy of the Holy Spirit.* Translated with an introduction by Joseph P. Farrell. Brookline, MA: Holy Cross Orthodox Press, 1987. 17-56.

Favier, Jean. *Philippe le Bel.* Paris: *Librairie Arthme Fayard*, 1978.

Foerster, Werner. *Gnosis: A Selection of Gnostic Texts.* 2 vols. English translation edited by R. McL. Wilson. Oxford: Clarendon Press, 1972.

Geanakoplos, Deno J. *Byzantine East and Latin West: Two Worlds of Christendom in Middle Ages and Renaissance: Studies in Ecclesiastical and Cultural History*. New York: Barnes and Noble, 1966.

Giles of Rome, *De Regimine principum libri III*. Rome: Stephan Plannck, 1482.

Grell, Ole Peter. Review of Pamela Smith. *The Business of Alchemy: Science and Culture in the Holy Roman Empire*. Princeton: Princeton University Press, 1994; and Raphael Patai. *The Jewish Alchemists: A History and Sourcebook*. Princeton: Princeton University Press, 1994. *The British Journal for the History of Science* 29.1 (March 1996): 93-94.

Griffiths, J. Gwyn. *Triads and Trinity*. Cardiff, Wales: University of Wales Press, 1996.

Guitton, Jean. "Leibniz and Pascal: Protestantinsm, Catholicism and Ecumenicism." *Cross Currents* 4.1 (Fall 1953): 12-35. Originally published in Jean Guitton. *Pascal et Leibniz: étude deux types de penseurs*. Paris: Aubier, 1951. 123-152.

Guthrie, W.K.C. *Orpheus and Greek Religion*. 2nd ed. London: Methuen, 1952.

Hadot, Pierre. *Le voile d'Isis. Essai sur l'histoire de l'idée de Nature*. Paris: Gallimard, 2004.

Halleux, Robert. *Les texts alchemiques*. Turnhout: Brepols, 1979.

Haugh, Richard. *Photius and the Carolingians: The Trinitarian Controversy*. Belmont, MA: Nordland, 1975.

Helvetius, John Friedrich. *The Golden Calf Which the World Adores and Desires....* London: Printed for John Starkey at the Mitre in Fleetstreet near Temple-Bar, 1670.

Heninger, S.K. *Touches of Sweet Harmony: Pythagorean Cosmology and Rensaissance Poetics*. San Marino, CA: The Huntington Library, 1974.

Henry, John. "Atomism and Eschatology: Catholicism and Natural Philosophy in the Interregnum." *British Journal for the History of Science* 15.3 (1982): 211-239.

Herd, Van Alan. *The Concept of Ungrund in Jakob Boehme (1575-1624)*. M.A. thesis, University of Oklahoma, 2003.

Hershbell, Jackson P. "Democritus and the Beginnings of Alchemy." *Ambix* 34.1 (March 1987): 5-20.

Hillgarth, J.N. *Ramon Lull and Lullism in Fourteenth-Century France*. Oxford: Clarendon Press, 1971.

Hobbes, Thomas. *The English Works of Thomas Hobbes of Malmesbury*. 11 vols. Ed. Sir William Molesworth. London, 1839-1845.

Holmyard, Eric John. *Alchemy*. New York: Courier Dover, 1990 (1957).

---. "Helvetius Meets an Adept." *Aryan Path* 2.10 (October 1931): 700-703.

Hooke, Sidney H. *Babylonian and Assyrian Religion*. Norman, OK: University of Oklahoma Press, 1963.

Hopkins, A.J. *Alchemy, Child of Greek Philosophy*. Morningside Heights, NY: Columbia University Press, 1934.

---. "A Study of the Kerotakis Process as Given by Zosimus and Later Alchemical Writers." *Isis* 29.2 (November, 1938): 326-354.

Horowicz, Mitch. *Occult America: The Secret History of How Mysticism Shaped Our Nation*. New York: Bantam, 2009.

Irby-Massie, Georgia, and Paul T. Keyser. *Greek Science of the Hellenistic Era: A Sourcebook*. London and New York: Routledge, 2002.

Jolley, Nicholas, ed. *The Cambridge Companion to Leibniz*. Cambridge: Cambridge University Press, 1995.

---. "Leibniz, Locke, and the Epistemology of Toleration." In *Leibniz and the English-Speaking World*. Ed. Pauline Phemister and Stuart C. Brown. Dordrecht, Netherlands: Springer, 2007. 133-143.

Jordan, G.J. *The Reunion of the Churches: A Study of G.W. Leibniz and His Great Attempt*. London: Constable and Co. Ltd., 1927.

Jung, C.G. *The Collected Works of C.G. Jung, Vol. 2. Psychology and Religion: East and West*. 2nd ed. Translated by R.F.C. Hull. Princeton, NJ: Princeton University Press, 1969.

Junker, Uwe, ed. Das "Buch der Heiligen Dreifaltigkeit." *Köln: Institut für Geschichte der Medizin der Universität*, 1986.

Kantorowicz, Ernst H. "'Feudalism' in the Byzantine Empire." In *Feudalism in History*. Ed. Rushton Coulborn. Hamden, CT: Archon Books, 1965. 151-166.

---. *The King's Two Bodies: A Study in Mediaeval Political Theology*. Princeton, NJ: Princeton University Press, 1957.

---. "Pro Patria Mori in Medieval Political Thought." *American Historical Review* 56.3 (April 1951): 472-492.

Karpenko, Valdimir. "Alchemy as *donum dei*." *Hyle—International Journal for Philosophy of Chemistry* 4.1 (1998). http://www.hyle.org/journal/issues/4/karpenk.htm.

---. "The Chemistry and Metallurgy of Transmutation." *Ambix* 39.2 (July 1992): 47-62.

---. "From Metals to Human Beings: Medical Aspects of European Alchemy." *Bulletin of the Indian Institute of the History of Medicine* 21.2 (1991): 105-119.

Kauffman, George B. "The Role of Gold in Alchemy. Part II." *Gold Bulletin* 18.2 (1985): 69-78.

---. "The Role of Gold in Alchemy. Part III." *Gold Bulletin* 18.3 (1985): 109-119.

Kelley, James L. *A Realism of Glory: Christology in the Works of Protopresbyter John Romanides*. Rollinsford, NH: Orthodox Research Institute, 2009.

Keyser, Paul T. "Alchemy in the Ancient World: From Science to Magic." *Illinois Classical Studies* 15 (1990): 353-378.

Kibre, Pearl. "The Intellectual Interests Reflected in Libraries of the 14C and 15C." *Journal of the History of Ideas* 7.3 (June 1946): 258-297.

Kingsley, Peter. *Ancient Philosophy, Mystery, and Magic: Empedocles and Pythagorean Tradition.* Oxford: Clarendon Press, 1995.

---. *In the Dark Places of Wisdom.* Inverness, CA: The Golden Sufi Center, 1999.

---. "Poimandres: The Etymology of the Name and the Origins of the Hermetica." In R. van den Broek and Cis van Heertum, eds. *From Poimandres to Jacob Böhme: Gnosis, Hermeticism and the Christian Tradition.* Amsterdam, The Netherlands: In de Pelikaan, 2000. 41-76.

Lach, Donald F. "Leibniz and China." *Journal of the History of Ideas* 6.4 (October 1945), 436-455.

Langlois, Charles-Victor. "Notices et documents relatifs à l'histoire du XIIe et du XIVe sicle: *Nova curie.*" *Revue historique* 87 (1905): 55-79.

LaVigne, Eric. "Squaring the Circle." *Parabola* 25.2 (May 2000): 34-41.

Leclerq, Dom Jean. "Un sermon prononcé pendant la guerre de Flandre sous Philippe le Bel." *Revue du moyen âge latin* 1 (1945): 165-172.

Leeuw, Gerardus Van der. *Religion in Essence and Manifestation.* Vol. 1. Translated by J.E. Turner. New York: Harper and Row, 1963.

Leibniz, G.W. *G. W. Leibniz: Discourse On Metaphysics and Related Writings.* Ed. R.N.D. Martin and Stuart Brown. Manchester and New York: Manchester University Press, 1988.

---. *G. W. Leibniz: Philosophical Texts.* Trans. Richard Francks and R.S. Woolhouse. Oxford: Oxford University Press, 1998.

---. *God. Guil. Leibnitii opera philosophica quae extant latine, gallica, germainica omnia.* Ed. J.E. Erdmann. Berlin, 1840.

---. *Gottfried Wilhelm Leibniz: Philosophical Papers and Letters.* Ed. Leroy E. Loemaker. 2 vols. Chicago: University of Chicago Press, 1956.

---. *Leibniz: Selections.* Ed. P. Wiener. New York: Charles Scribner's Sons, 1951.

---. *Samtliche Schriften und Briefe.* Ed. Academy of Sciences of Berlin, Series I-VIII. Darmstadt, Leipzig, and Berlin, 1923ff.

Lewis, Andrew W. *Royal Succession in Capetian France: Studies on Familial Order and the State.* Cambridge, MA and London: Harvard University Press, 1981.

Lindsay, Jack. *The Origins of Alchemy in Graeco-Roman Egypt.* New York: Barnes and Noble, Inc., 1970.

---. *Origins of Astrology.* New York: Barnes and Noble, 1971.

Lloyd, G.E.R. *Polarity and Analogy: Two Types of Argumentation in Early Greek Thought.* Cambridge: Cambridge University Press, 1966.

Loemaker, Leroy E. "Leibniz and the Herborn Encyclopedists," *Journal of the History of Ideas* 22.3 (July-Sept 1961): 323-338.

Louthan, Howard. "Introduction." In *John Comenius: The Labyrinth of the World and the Paradise of the Heart*. Mahwah, NJ: Paulist Press, 1998. 7-54.

Lovejoy, A.O. *The Great Chain of Being*. Cambridge and London: Harvard University Press, 1964.

Macdonald Ross, G. *Leibniz*. Oxford: Oxford University Press, 1984.

Mahdihassan, Syed. "Alchemy and Its Chinese Origin As Revealed by Its Etymology, Doctrines and Symbols." *Iqbal Review* 7 (1966): 22-58.

---. "Alchemy and Its Fundamental Terms in Greek, Arabic, Sanskrit, and Chinese." *Indian Journal of History of Science* 16.1 (May 1981): 64-76.

---. "Alchemy, Chinese Versus Greek, An Etymological Approach: A Rejoinder." *American Journal of Chinese Medicine* 16.1-2 (1988): 83-86.

---. "Alchemy, in Its Proper Setting, with Jinn, Sufi, and Suffa, as Loan-Words form the Chinese." *Iqbal* 7.3 (1959): 1-10.

---. "Alchemy in the Light of Jung's Psychology and of Dualism." *The Pakistan Philosophical Journal* 5 (1962): 95-103.

---. "Cinnabar-gold as the Best Alchemical Drug of Longevity, Called Makaradhwaja in India." *American Journal of Chinese Medicine* 13 (1985): 93-108.

---. "Creation, Its Nature and Imitation in Alchemy." *Iqbal Review* 9 (1968): 80-115.

---. "Dualistic Symbolism, Alchemical and Masonic." *Iqbal* 12.1 (1963): 55-70.

---. *Indian Alchemy or Rasayana in the Light of Asceticism and Geriatrics*. New Delhi: Vikas, 1979.

---. "Jabir's Magic Square as the Symbol of Venus Which Was the Eight Cornered Star," *Hamdard Medicus* 34.3 (July-September 1991): 46-48.

---. "Ouroboros as the Earliest Symbol of Greek Alchemy." *Iqbal* 9 (1961): 1-21.

---. "Outline of the Beginnings of Alchemy and It's Antecedents." *American Journal of Chinese Medicine* 12 (1984): 32-42.

---. "A Positive Conception of the Divinity Emanating from a Study of Alchemy." *Iqbal Review* 10 (1969): 77-125.

---. "The Seven Theories Identifying the Soma Plant." *Ancient Science of Life* 9.2 (October 1989): 86-89.

---. "The Significance of Ouroboros in Alchemy and Primitive Symbolism." *Iqbal* 12 (1963): 18-47.

Maier, M. *Atalanta fugiens*. Oppenheim, 1618.

Matus, Zachary Alexander. *Heaven in a Bottle: Franciscan Apolcalypticism and the Elixir, 1250-1360*. PhD dissertation. Cambridge, MA: Harvard University, 2010.

May, William E. "The God of Leibniz." *New Scholasticism* 36 (1962): 506-528.

McEvilley, Thomas. *The Shape of Ancient Thought: Comparative Studies in Greek and Indian Philosophies.* New York: Allworth Press, 2002.

McGuckin, John. *Standing in God's Holy Fire: The Byzantine Tradition.* London: Darton, Longman and Todd, 2001.

McKenna, Terence. *Food of the Gods: The Search for the Original Tree of Knowledge, A Radical History of Plants, Drugs, and Human Evolution.* New York: Bantam, 1992.

Mendelsohn, J. Andrew. "Alchemy and Politics in England, 1649-1665." *Past and Present* 135 (May 1992): 30-78.

Mercer, Christia. *Leibniz's Metaphysics: Its Origins and Development.* Cambridge: Cambridge University Press, 2001.

Mertens, Michèle. "Graeco-Egyptian Alchemy in Byzantium." Avail. online at: http://orbi.ulg.ac.be/bitstream/2268/14188/1/205-230%20M.%20 Mertens1.pdf.

Merton, Robert K. *Science, Technology and Society in Seventeenth-Century England.* New York: Harper and Row, 1970. Originally published in *Osiris* 4.2 (1938): 414-565.

Meyendorff, John. *Imperial Unity and Christian Divisions.* Crestwood, NY: St. Vladimir's Orthodox Seminary Press, 1989.

Migne, J.-P., ed. *Patrologia Latino.* 221 vols. Paris, 1844-55.

Modi, Jivanji Jamshedji. *The Religious Ceremonies and Customs of the Parsees.* Mazagon, Bombay: British India Press, 1922.

Moran, Bruce T. *Distilling Knowledge: Alchemy, Chemistry, and the Scientific Revolution.* Cambridge, MA and London: Harvard University Press, 2005.

Müller, Kurt. *Leibniz-Bibliographie: die Literatur über Leibniz bis 1980.* Frankfurt am Main: Vittorio Klostermann, 1984.

---. *Leibniz-Bibliographie, Band 2. Die Literatur über Leibniz, 1981-1990.* Frankfurt am Main: Vittorio Klostermann, 1996.

Munnis, Jeff. "Peter Kingsley and the Discomfort of Wisdom." *AntiMatters* 1.2 (2007): 143-153.

Nadler, Stephen. *The Best of All Possible Worlds: A Story of Philosophers, God, and Evil.* New York: Farrar, Straus and Giroux, 2008.

Needham, Joseph. *Science and Civilisation in China, Volume 5. Chemistry and Chemical Technology, Part 2. Spagyrical Discovery and Invention: Magisteries of Gold and Immortality.* Cambridge: Cambridge University Press, 1974.

Nelson, Janet L. "National Synods, Kingship as Office, and Royal Anointing: An Early Medieval Syndrome." In *Politics and Ritual in Early Medieval Europe.* London and Ronceverte: Hambledon Press, 1986. 239-281. Originally published in *Studies in Church History* 13 (1976): 97-119.

Newman, William. *Gehennical Fire: The Lives of George Starkey, an American Alchemist in the Scientific Revolution.* Chicago and London: University of Chicago Press, 2002.

---. *Promethean Ambitions: Alchemy and the Quest to Perfect Nature.* Chicago and London: University of Chicago Press, 2004.

O'Flaherty, Wendy Doniger, ed. and trans. *The Rig Veda: An Anthology.* London: Penguin, 1981.

Ogrinc, Will H.L. "Western Society and Alchemy from 1200 to 1500." *Journal of Medieval History* 6 (1980): 103-132.

Orio de Miguel, Bernardo. "Some Hermetic Aspects of Leibniz's Mathematical Rationalism." In *Leibniz: What Kind of Rationalist?* Ed. Marcelo Dascal. New York: Springer, 2008. 111-124.

Pagel, Walter. "Jung's Views On Alchemy." *Isis* 39 (1948): 44-48.

---. "Paracelsus and the Neoplatonic and Gnostic Tradition." *Ambix* 8.3 (1960): 125-166.

de Pange, Jean. *Le Roi Très Chrétien.* Paris: Librairie Arthème Fayard, 1949.

Papadakis, Ariseides, and John Meyendorff. *The Christian East and the Rise of the Papacy.* Crestwood, NY: St. Vladimir's Seminary Press, 1994.

Paracelsus. *The Aurora of the Philosophers, from Paracelsus, his Aurora and Treasure of the Philosophers, As also The Water-Stone of the Wise Men; Describing the matter of, and manner hot to attain the universal Tincture. Faithfully Englished, and Published by J.H. Oxon.* London: Giles Calver, 1659.

Patai, Raphael. *The Jewish Alchemists: A History and Sourcebook.* Princeton: Princeton University Press, 1994.

Pereira, Michela. "Alchemy and Hermeticism: An Introduction To This Issue." *Early Science and Medicine* 5.2 (2000): 115-120.

---. "William Newman, *Promethean Ambitions: Alchemy and the Quest to Perfect Nature* (Review)." *Renaissance Quarterly* 58.2 (Summer, 2005): 678-680.

Pertz, G.H., ed. *Monumenta Germaniae Historica. Libelli de lite imperatorum et pontificum.* Hanover: Hahn, 1891-1897.

Plass, Paul. "A Greek Alchemical Formula." *Ambix* 29.2 (July 1982): 69-73.

Plato: Complete Works. Ed. John M. Cooper. Indianapolis, IN: Hackett, 1997.

Plotinus. *Enneads III.* Loeb Classical Library no. 442. Ed. and translated by Arthur Hilary Armstrong. Cambridge, MA and London: Harvard University Press, 1967.

Plowden, Edmund. *Commentaries, or Reports of Edmund Plowden.* London: S. Brooke, Paternoster Row, 1816 (1571).

Polanyi, Michael. *Knowing and Being.* Chicago: University of Chicago Press, 1969.

Politella, J. *Platonism, Aristotelianism, and Cabalism in the Philosophy of Leibniz.* Philadelphia: University of Pennsylvania, 1938.

Pregadio, Fabrizio. "Alchemy. China." In *New Dictionary of the History of Ideas.* Ed. Maryanne Cline Horowitz. 6 vols. Detroit: Thompson Gale, 2005. 1.38-40.

---.   *Great Clarity: Daoism and Alchemy in Early Medieval China.* Stanford, CA: Stanford University Press, 2006.

Principe, Lawrence M., and William R. Newman, "Some Problems with the Historiography of Alchemy." In *Secrets of Nature: Astrology and Alchemy in Early Modern Europe.* Ed. William R. Newman and Anthony Grafton. Cambridge, MA: MIT Press, 2001. 387-431.

Quasten, Johannes. *Patrology.* 4 vols. Utrecht and Antwerp: Spectrum Publishers; Westminster, MD: Newman Press and Christian Classics, 1966-1994.

Raven, J.E. *Pythagoreans and Eleatics: An Account of the Interaction Between the Two Opposed Schools During the Fifth and Early Fourth Centuries B.C.* Amsterdam: Adolf M. Hakkert, 1966.

Ridgeway, Sir William. "What Led Pythagoras to the Doctrine That the World Was Built of Numbers?" *Classical Review* 10.2 (March, 1896): 92-95.

Roberts, A., and J. Donaldson, eds. *The Ante-Nicene Fathers.* 10 vols. New York, 1926 (1885-1887).

Romanides, John S. *The Ancestral Sin.* Translated with an introduction by George S. Gabriel. Ridgewood: Zephyr, 2002.

---.   "The Christological Teaching of John of Damascus." *Ekklesiastikos Pharos* 58 (1976): 232-269.

---.   *An Outline of Orthodox Patristic Dogmatics.* Translated by George Dion. Dragas. Rollinsford, NH: Orthodox Research Institute, 2004.

---.   www.romanity.org. Last accessed 9 April, 2009.

---.   *Romeosyne, Romania, Rumeli.* Thessolaniki, Greece: Pournara, 1974.

---.   "Yahweh of Glory According to the 1st, 2nd, and 9th Ecumenical Councils." *Theologia* 71 (2000): 133-199.

Roob, Alexander. *The Hermetic Museum: Alchemy and Mysticism.* Köln: Tachen, 1997.

Rundle Clark, R.T. *Myth and Symbol in Ancient Egypt.* London: Thames and Hudson, 1959.

Said, Hakim Mohammed, ed. *Essays On Science: Felicitation Volume in Honour of Dr. S. Mahdihassan.* Karachi, Pakistan: Hamdard Foundation Press, 1987.

Saluste du Bartas, Guillaume. His *Devine Weekes and Works.* Translated by Joshua Sylvester. 1605; repr., Gainesville, FL: Scholars' Facsimiles and Reprints, 1965.

Sarton, George. Review of Julius Ruska. *Tabula Smaragdina. Isis* 9.2 (June, 1927): 375-377.

Schwaller De Lubicz, R.A. *Sacred Science: The King of Pharaonic Theocracy.* Rochester, VT: Inner Traditions International, 1988.

Scott, Walter. *Hermetica: The Ancient Greek and Latin Writings Which Contain Religious or Philosophic Teachings Ascribed to Hermes Trismegistus,*

Vol. 1: Introduction, Texts and Translations. Boston, MA: Shambhala, 1985 (1924).

Sheppard, HJ . "Alchemy: Origin or Origins?" *Ambix* 17.2 (July 1970): 69-84.

---.   "European Alchemy in the Context of a Universal Definition." In *Die Alchemie in der europaischen Kultur- und wissenschaftsgeschichte.* Wiesbaden: Otto Harrassowitz, 1986. 13-17.

---.   "The Ouroboros and the Unity of Matter in Alchemy." *Ambix* 10 (1962): 83-96.

Sherrard, Philip. *Church, Papacy and Schism: A Theological Enquiry.* Limnia, Evia, Greece: Denise Harvey, 1996 (1976).

Silberer, Herbert. *Hidden Symbolism of Alchemy and the Occult Arts.* Translated by Smith Ely Jelliffe. New York: Dover, 1971 (1917).

Sopko, Andrew J. *Prophet of Roman Orthodoxy: The Theology of John Romanides.* Dewdney, B.C.: Synaxis Press, 1998.

Spiegel, Gabrielle M. "'Defense of the Realm': Evolution of a Capetian Propaganda Slogan." *Journal of Medieval History* 3 (1977): 115-134.

Stapleton, H.E., and G.J.W. "Ancient and Modern Aspects of Pythagoreanism." *Osiris* 13 (1958): 12-53.

Strayer, Joseph R. "Defense of the Realm and Royal Power in France." In *Studi in orore di Gino Luzzato.* 2 vols. Milan, 1949. 1.289-296.

---.   "France: the Holy Land, the Chosen People and the Most Christian King" In *Medieval Statecraft and the Perspectives of History: Essays by Joseph R. Strayer.* Ed. J. F. Benton and T. H. Bisson. Princeton, NJ: Princeton University Press, 1971. 300-314.

---.   "The Laicization of French and English Society in the Thirteenth Century." *Speculum* 15.1 (Jan. 1940): 76-86.

---.   "Philip the Fair—A 'Constitutional' King." *American Historical Review* 62.1 (October, 1956): 18-32.

---.   *The Reign of Philip the Fair.* Princeton, NJ: Princeton University Press, 1980.

von Stuckrad, Kocku. "Recent Studies On Western Esotericism: Some Reflections." *Numen* 49 (2002): 212-218.

Szulakowska, Ursula. "Patronage in Relation to Alchemical Illustration in the Early Italian Renaissance: Three Case Studies." *Artium Academiae Scintiarium Hungaricae* 35 (1990/1992): 169-180.

Taylor, F.S. *The Alchemists.* New York: Henry Schuman, 1949.

Te-K'un, Cheng. "Yin-Yang Wu-Hsing and Han Art." *Harvard Journal of Asiatic Studies* 20 (1957): 162-186.

Tillich, Paul. *A History of Christian Thought.* New York, 1968.

---.   *Systematic Theology.* 3 vols. Chicago: University of Chicago Press, 1963.

Ullmann, Walter. *The Growth of Papal Government in the Middle Ages: A Study in the Ideological Relation of Clerical to Lay Power.* 3rd ed. London: Methuen, 1970 (1955).

---.   *A Short History of the Papacy in the Middle Ages.* 2nd ed. London: Routledge, 2003 (1972).

Utke, A.R. "Alchemy and the Concept of Ultimate Reality and Meaning." *Ultimate Reality and Meaning* 27.1 (2004): 51-69.

---.   "The Cosmic Holism Concept: An Interdisciplinary Tool In the Quest For Ultimate Reality and Meaning." *Interdisciplinary Studies In the Understanding of Ultimate Reality and Meaning* 17.3 (1986): 134-155.

Vennebusch, Joachim. *Gottfried Wilhelm Leibniz: Philosopher and Politician in the Service of a Universal Culture.* Bad Godesberg, Germany: Inter Nationes, 1966.

Waite, A.E., ed. *The Hermetic Museum,* 2 vols. London: J. Elliot and Co., 1893.

Walker, D.P. "The Astral Body in Renaissance Medicine." *Journal of the Warburg and Courtauld Institutes* 21.1/2 (Jan.-Jun. 1958): 119-133.

White, David Gordon. *The Alchemical Body: Siddha Traditions in Medieval India.* Chicago and London: University of Chicago Press, 1996.

Wilson, C. Anne. "Pythagorean Theory and Dionysian Practice: The Cultic and Practical Background To Chemical Experimentation in Hellenistic Egypt." *Ambix* 45.1 (March 1998): 14-33.

---.   *Philosophers, Iōsis and Water of Life.* Leeds: W.S. Maney and Son Ltd., 1984.

Wilson, Catherine. "Leibniz and Atomism." *Studies in History and Philosophy of Science* 15 (1982): 175-199.

Wheelwright, Phillip. *The Burning Fountain: A Study of the Language of Symbolism.* Bloomington: Indiana University Press, 1968.

Woodward, Walter W. "The Alchemy of Alchemy." *The William and Mary Quarterly* 60.4 (2003): 920-924.

Yates, Francis A. *Giordano Bruno and the Hermetic Tradition.* Chicago: University of Chicago Press, 1964.

---.   "The Hermetic Tradition in Renaissance Science." In *Art, Science, and History in the Renaissance.* Ed. Charles S. Singleton. Baltimore: Johns Hopkins Press, 1967. 227-246.

Zosimos of Panopolis. "The Visions of Zosimos." Translated by F. Sherwood Taylor. *Ambix* 1 (1937): 88-92.